From Muffins To Margaritas

Visit the Kitchens
of Florida's Finest Inns

Dedicated to Herb Hiller

It was mid-morning of February in the 1960s, and I was working in our office, when a nice-looking individual with a longish hairstyle and light beard appeared, approaching the office with no visible means of transportation. We needed a pot washer at that time, and our good fortune continued, it would seem, as he appeared to be walking right into the office.

Herb Hiller, the writer, was a long way from dishwashing. He was touring Florida and had come from Miami on his bicycle, gathering material for his book by stopping at small inns all over Florida. It was through his boundless and tireless energy and enthusiasm that the association of Inn Route was born. In his write-up for us, he featured a little sign we had on the piano, which read, "Please play anything except 'Chopsticks.' " Herb certainly played everything into the hearts and minds and memory of his coordinated creation of the Inn Route association. Many thanks to him for this.

Robert C. Buffum
Manasota Beach Club
Englewood, Florida

From **Muffins** to **Margaritas**

Copyright © 1999
Inn Route
P.O. Box 6187
Palm Harbor, Florida 34684
800-524-1880
www.florida-inns.com

Library of Congress Catalog Number: 98-075108
ISBN: 0-9665907-0-8

Edited, Designed and Manufactured by Favorite Recipes® Press
an imprint of

P.O. Box 305142, Nashville, Tennessee 37230, (800) 358-0560

Manufactured in the United States of America
First Printing: 1999
6,500 copies

Table of Contents

Tallahassee and The Panhandle

Magnolias, history, and Southern hospitality somehow set Florida's capital apart from the rest of the state. At the northern edge of the state, Tallahassee is often described as its most Southern city. The streets are narrower and the pace is slower. Small towns dot the area, waiting to come alive for fall football games.

To Tallahassee's west, the Florida Panhandle is known for its sugar-white beaches of quartz sand and emerald green waters. The Gulf Island National Seashore protects twenty-two miles of coastline, making this region one of the most pristine in the country. Panhandle beaches are regularly listed among the best in America. Set apart from the rest of the state, both by its geography and climate, this region thrives as a summertime family destination.

Florida
Panhandle

Santa Rosa Beach

Chocolate Chunk Coffee Cake Muffins

4 ounces German's chocolate, chopped
½ cup chopped nuts
1¼ cups sugar
1 teaspoon cinnamon
1¾ cups flour
½ teaspoon baking powder
¼ teaspoon salt
1 cup sour cream
1 teaspoon baking soda
½ cup margarine, softened
2 eggs
½ teaspoon vanilla extract

Preheat the oven to 400 degrees. Combine the chocolate, nuts, ¼ cup of the sugar and cinnamon in a small bowl and mix well. Set aside. Combine the flour, baking powder and salt in a bowl and mix well. Combine the sour cream and baking soda in a bowl and mix well. Cream the margarine and remaining 1 cup sugar in a bowl until light and fluffy. Add the eggs 1 at a time, mixing well after each addition. Add the vanilla and mix well. Add the dry ingredients alternately with the sour cream mixture, beginning and ending with the dry ingredients and blending well after each addition. Spoon half the batter into 12 greased muffin cups. Top with half the nut mixture. Repeat the layers. Bake for 20 to 25 minutes or until muffins begin to pull away from sides of muffin cups.

Yield: 12 muffins

Seafood and Vegetable Crepes

1 cup flour
¼ teaspoon salt
½ cup milk
½ cup water
2 extra-large eggs
1 tablespoon vegetable oil, or
   2 tablespoons butter, melted
2 summer squash
2 zucchini
½ eggplant
2 tablespoons olive oil
½ teaspoon garlic salt
¼ teaspoon pepper
2 pinches dry basil
2 pinches dillweed
2 plum tomatoes, peeled
4 sticks imitation crab meat
Lemon dill sauce to taste

Combine the flour, salt, milk, water and eggs in a bowl and whisk just until smooth. Refrigerate, covered, for 2 hours to overnight. Brush the bottom of an 8-inch crepe pan with vegetable oil. Heat over medium heat until bubbly. Pour a scant ¼ cup of the batter into the pan. Tilt the pan to coat the bottom with the oil. Cook for 1 to 2 minutes or until top is set and underside is browned. Turn over and cook other side until light brown. Remove to a warm platter. Repeat with the remaining batter. Peel and coarsely chop the summer squash, zucchini and eggplant. Heat olive oil in a large pan over medium heat. Add summer squash, zucchini, eggplant, garlic salt, pepper, basil and dillweed. Sauté for 10 minutes. Reduce the heat and simmer. Chop the tomatoes and crab meat. Add to the vegetables. Cook until heated through. Fill each crepe with 1½ teaspoons of the mixture and roll up. Serve with lemon dill sauce.

Yield: 4 servings

A Highlands House Bed & Breakfast Inn

Joan and Ray Robins
Scenic 30A
Santa Rosa Beach, Florida 32459
(850) 267-0110

A Highlands House is a charming escape reminiscent of times and places long forgotten. This antebellum-style home affords each guest comfort, privacy, and direct access to the best beaches in Florida.

Close to Seaside and Destin, A Highlands House has received national recognition in Florida Living Magazine; Frommers Florida; America's Favorite Inns, B&B, & Small Hotels; and others.

What makes Seaside unique
is its quiet simplicity. There is a
sense of comfort and security
within the brick-lined streets and
white picket fences. It is
reminiscent of a bygone era, when
couples strolled hand-in-hand
and children played freely in the
parks. The sounds of the surf, sea
gulls, and free outdoor concerts
abound. If the fantasy of an
idyllic lifestyle appeals to you, this
is surely the place to find it.

Chef Bruce's Seafood Althinean

For a one-person serving, Chef Bruce uses a 6-ounce portion of Scamp, his personal favorite local fish. However, any fish of choice could be substituted. To accommodate more guests, just multiply the ingredients accordingly.

1 (6- to 8-ounce) portion of fish
2 ounces white wine
Olive oil to taste
Juice of ½ fresh lemon
Pinch of salt and coarsely
    ground pepper
Sprig of fresh thyme
2 tablespoons chopped fresh basil
1 teaspoon minced garlic
1 tablespoon butter (optional)
4 canned unmarinated
    artichoke hearts
5 ounces fresh spinach
1 serving hot cooked
    angel hair pasta
Steamed vegetables of choice

Preheat the oven to 350 degrees. Place the fish in a small baking dish. Combine the wine, olive oil, lemon juice, salt, pepper, thyme, basil, garlic and butter in a small bowl and mix well. Pour over the fish. Place 2 artichoke hearts on each side of the fish. Bake the fish for 20 to 30 minutes or until cooked through. Wilt the spinach in a small amount of olive oil and a dash of white wine in a small sauté pan. Place the pasta in the center of the serving plate. Place the wilted spinach and fish over the pasta. Surround with the artichoke hearts and steamed vegetables. Drizzle the sauce from the baking dish over the top. Garnish with a fresh basil sprig and lemon wedge.

Yield: 1 serving

Jack-Berry-Jo Strata

This double-stuffed French toast baked in the oven works great for special occasion brunches and holiday get-togethers. It is assembled the night before, so the "Chef" has plenty of time to spend with guests the day of the function.

2 (20-slice) loaves white bread

12 eggs

4 cups heavy cream or milk

1 (16-ounce) jar strawberry jam

1 pound Monterey Jack cheese,
   shredded

¼ cup butter

2 tablespoons (about) flour

½ cup (about) heavy cream

2 tablespoons rum extract

½ cup (about) strawberry jam

3 fresh kiwifruit, chopped

1 pint fresh strawberries, chopped

1 mango, chopped

Confectioners' sugar

Shaved chocolate

Cut the white bread into small cubes. Combine eggs and 4 cups cream in a large bowl and mix well. Add bread cubes and stir until the bread is coated. Place half the bread mixture in a 9x12-inch baking pan sprayed with nonstick cooking spray. Spread 16 ounces strawberry jam over the bread mixture. Sprinkle the cheese over the jam. Top with the remaining bread mixture. Chill, covered, in the refrigerator for 8 to 10 hours. Preheat the oven to 350 degrees. Place the baking pan in a larger baking pan. Pour the hottest tap water into the larger baking pan to a depth of 1 inch. Bake for 1 hour or until the center is firm to the touch. Melt butter in the top of a double boiler over hot but not boiling water. Whisk in enough of the flour to thicken. Stir in enough of the ½ cup heavy cream until of desired consistency. Stir in rum extract and ½ cup strawberry jam. Cook over low heat for 25 minutes, stirring occasionally. Cut strata into individual serving squares. Place a ladle of sauce on the center of each serving plate. Place strata square in center of sauce. Sprinkle with kiwifruit, strawberries and mango. Dust with confectioners' sugar and shaved chocolate.

Yield: 12 servings

Josephine's French Country Inn

Bruce and Jody Albert

P.O. Box 4767

Seaside, Florida 32459

(800) 848-1840

Josephine's French Country Inn offers romantic getaways in a fairytale setting unequaled in the Florida Panhandle. Seven beautifully appointed rooms and two luxurious suites complete with fireplaces, bathtubs-for-two, and full amenities await you. Bruce and Judy Albert add a warmth reminiscent of the old-style bed-and-breakfasts, but with all the modern conveniences of finer establishments worldwide. For your ultimate dining pleasure, most of the fresh vegetables and herbs served in their intimate, four-star dining room are organically grown on the Albert's local farm.

Apalachicola

Get a taste of timelessness in Apalachicola (Land of Friendly People), which offers history and maritime culture, along with a strong art-based community that complements the area's bountiful natural resources. The unique nature of the Apalachicola Bay's estuary accommodates both fresh and saltwater fishing buffs.

Off-shore scuba diving enthusiasts can explore underwater reefs and artifacts. Land lovers can spend time browsing through the city's art galleries and antique shops, or touring the Apalachicola National Estuarine Research Reserve (a marine research facility), St. Vincent's Island Office, and the renowned John Gorrie State Museum. Be sure to stop by the Apalachicola Maritime Museum, where you can purchase tickets to sail into the evening aboard the historic sailing schooner, the Governor Stone.

Barnzys Banana Bread

½ cup butter, melted
1 cup sugar
2 eggs
¾ cup mashed ripe banana
1 ¼ cups flour
¾ teaspoon baking soda
½ teaspoon salt
¼ cup butter, melted
½ cup packed brown sugar

Preheat the oven to 350 degrees. Combine ½ cup butter, sugar, eggs and banana in a bowl and mix well. Combine the flour, baking soda and salt in a bowl and mix well. Stir into the banana mixture. Pour into a greased loaf pan. Bake for 30 to 35 minutes or until the loaf tests done. Combine ¼ cup melted butter and brown sugar in a bowl and mix well. Spread on top of the hot baked bread.

Note: This recipe also makes great muffins. Spoon the batter into greased muffin cups. Place 1 teaspoon of grape, raspberry or strawberry jelly in the center of each and bake. Makes a great sweet center.

Yield: 1 loaf

Tupelo Honey Oatmeal

1 or 2 Yellow Delicious apples,
   peeled, cut
5 to 10 dashes of cinnamon
4 to 7 dashes of salt
½ cup raisins
½ cup mashed pecans
½ cup Tupelo Honey
Small pieces of pineapple
   (optional)
Quick-cooking rolled oats

Combine the apples, cinnamon, salt, raisins, pecans, Tupelo Honey, pineapple and enough water to make desired amount of oatmeal in a large saucepan. Let stand for 8 to 10 hours. Bring to a boil. Boil for 3 to 4 minutes, stirring often. Add the desired amount of oats. Reduce the heat to low. Cover and keep warm until ready to serve, adding milk or water as needed to keep moist.

Note: Ever wonder what to do with the hard center core of a pineapple? Well, when preparing this recipe just place the core in the water mixture and let the juices seep out during the standing process. After bringing the mixture to a boil you can remove the core of the pineapple and add the oats.

Yield: variable

The Coombs House Inn
Pamela Barnes and Anthony Erario
Number 80, 6th Street
Apalachicola, Florida 32320
(850) 653-9199

A three-story Victorian mansion restored with charm and authenticity, this elegant bed-and-breakfast in Apalachicola's Historic District offers complimentary continental breakfast, cable TV, and air conditioning. It is just minutes from pristine beaches on St. George Island, superb fishing, and boating. Discover this pearl along Florida's final frontier. You'll find eighteen rooms in two buildings, bicycles, and Jacuzzis.

Havana

Located twelve miles north of
Tallahassee and founded in 1906,
Havana, Florida was named after
Havana, Cuba. A premium
grade of cigar wrapper tobacco
was the connection. With the
demise of that major crop, so fell
the downtown area. Today,
instead of empty stores, Main
Street again bustles with
shoppers. Flowers and trees
bloom. Within easy walking
distance, there are several streets
lined with cafés, antique
shops, and shops filled with
collectibles and gifts.

Historic Havana House Grand Granola

8 cups old-fashioned rolled oats
1½ cups packed brown sugar
1½ cups untoasted wheat germ
1½ cups chopped unsalted pecans
1½ cups unprocessed oat bran
½ cup untoasted sesame seeds
½ cup unsalted sunflower seeds
½ cup canola oil
¾ cup honey
2 teaspoons vanilla extract
2 cups raisins

Preheat the oven to 325 degrees. Combine the
oats, brown sugar, wheat germ, pecans, bran,
sesame seeds and sunflower seeds in a bowl
and mix well. Set aside. Combine the oil,
honey and vanilla in a small saucepan. Bring
to a boil. Pour over the dry ingredients, stirring
constantly. Mix thoroughly. Spread the mixture
in a large shallow baking pan sprayed with
nonstick cooking spray. Bake for 30 minutes,
stirring every 5 minutes. Remove from oven.
Stir every 5 minutes until cooled completely.
Stir in the raisins. May be stored in sealable
plastic bags in the freezer for several months.

Yield: 14 to 15 cups

Bodacious Banana Nut Bread with Topping Historic Havana Style

2½ cups self-rising flour

1 cup sugar

1 cup mashed ripe bananas
    (2 to 3 medium)

3 tablespoons canola oil

¾ cup milk

1 egg, or 2 egg whites

1¼ cups finely chopped pecans

Topping (below)

Preheat the oven to 350 degrees. Grease and flour a 5x9-inch loaf pan or two 4½x8½-inch loaf pans. Combine the flour, sugar, bananas, oil, milk, egg and 1 cup of the pecans in a mixer bowl. Beat at medium speed for 30 seconds or until well mixed. Pour into the prepared pan. Bake for 55 to 65 minutes or until a wooden pick inserted in the center comes out clean. Cool in the pan on a wire rack for 10 minutes. Invert onto the wire rack to cool completely. Spread with the Topping. Sprinkle with remaining ¼ cup pecans.

Yield: 1 loaf

Topping

1 ripe medium banana, mashed

1¼ cups sifted
    confectioners' sugar

1 teaspoon lemon juice

Cream the banana, confectioners' sugar and lemon juice in a bowl.

Yield: 1½ cups

Historic Havana House

Bruce and Shirley Gaver
301 East Sixth Avenue
Havana, Florida 32333
(850) 539-5611

Located one block from Havana's Antique and Art District with its 50 shops, Gaver's 1907 home has tongue-and-groove wooden walls, twelve-foot ceilings, and a private art collection. Both rooms, one with a queen-size cherry canopy bed and the other with wicker twin beds (or a king-size bed), have private baths. Early morning coffee is served on the screened porch and in the garden pergola. Full country gourmet breakfast is served. Tallahassee and Florida State University are minutes away.

Milton

Beautiful snow white Gulf beaches, Pensacola, a well-preserved and interesting historic city, the "Cradle of Naval Aviation," and the Naval Aviation Museum—all these and more attract visitors to fascinating Northwest Florida. Adjacent to Pensacola, in Milton, "The Canoe Capital" of Florida, is the Adventures Unlimited Outdoor Center, home of the Wolfe Creek Schoolhouse Bed & Breakfast Inn. At the Outdoor Center, visitors can enjoy canoeing, tubing, kayaking, a hayride, or challenge ropes adventure. The clear, sand beach-laced streams flow through the Blackwater River State Forest, the largest state forest in Florida. Biking is also available on the newly completed Blackwater Heritage Rail To Trail in Milton.

Creekside Kitchen's Easy Banana Nut Muffins

½ *cup shortening*
1 *cup sugar*
2 *eggs*
1½ *cups mashed bananas*
2 *cups flour*
1 *teaspoon cinnamon*
1 *teaspoon baking soda*
½ *cup pecan pieces*
1 *cup (about) buttermilk*

Preheat the oven to 325 degrees. Cream the shortening and sugar in a large mixer bowl until light and fluffy. Add the eggs and bananas and mix well. Stir in the flour, cinnamon, baking soda and pecans. Add buttermilk just until a thick batter forms, stirring constantly. Spoon the batter into 6 jumbo muffin cups. Bake for 15 minutes or until the muffins test done.

Yield: 6 jumbo muffins

Adventure Rolls

These are our version of "sin"amon rolls.

7 cups (about) flour
1/2 cup sugar
2 teaspoons salt
4 1/2 teaspoons dry yeast
1 cup milk
1 cup water
1/2 cup butter
Cinnamon to taste
Sugar to taste
1 pound confectioners' sugar
1/3 cup (about) milk
2 teaspoons vanilla extract

Combine 2 cups of the flour, sugar, salt and yeast in a large bowl. Heat 1 cup milk, water and butter in a small saucepan until the butter is melted, stirring to mix. Add the milk mixture to the flour mixture and mix well. Stir in 2 1/2 to 3 cups of the flour. Remove the dough to a floured surface. Spray the bowl with nonstick cooking spray; set aside. Knead the dough for 5 minutes or until the dough is soft and elastic, adding up to 2 cups of the flour. Return the dough to the prepared bowl. Cover loosely with a tea towel. Let rise in a warm place until doubled in bulk. Spray a baking sheet with nonstick cooking spray. Punch down the dough. Remove to a floured surface and roll out into a large rectangle. Spread the dough with the butter. Sprinkle with cinnamon and sugar. Roll as for a jellyroll, pinching the edges to seal. Cut into 1 1/2-inch-thick slices. Arrange about 1 inch apart on the prepared baking sheet. Let rise in a warm place for 40 minutes or until doubled in bulk. Preheat the oven to 375 degrees. Bake for 30 minutes or until light golden brown. Combine the confectioners' sugar, vanilla and enough of the 1/3 cup milk to make of glaze consistency in a small bowl and mix well. Spread over the warm rolls. Serve immediately or let stand to cool completely before wrapping individually in plastic wrap.

Yield: 30 rolls

**Adventures Unlimited
Schoolhouse Inn**
Jack and Esther Sanborn
Route 6, Box 283
Milton, Florida 32570
(850) 623-6197

Originally the Schoolhouse Inn served as a four-room school in the Fidelis Community, 22 miles north of Milton. The school was completed in 1926 and served as a primary school for grades K-8 until the end of the 1984-85 school year. Now, the Schoolhouse Inn has eight spacious, individual rooms with private baths. The rooms have twelve-foot ceilings, pecan and oak hardwood floors, and beaded walls that are in keeping with the old schoolhouse charm. The rooms are themed after prominent American authors. The essences of the authors, along with their works, are captured in the décor and atmosphere of each room. So come relax in a rocker or swing on the front porch, read a book, and slip back to another era.

Historic Northeast Florida

Where it all started...time has not stood still.
Out of America's beginnings in the history of
St. Augustine and Fernandina Beach, rose
Jacksonville, one of Florida's largest cities,
divided by the long and winding St. John's
River. Magnificent wide, golden
sand beaches are a constant
throughout this diverse
coastline. St. Augustine offers our
country's first history—cobblestone
streets, horse-drawn carriages, and
attractions galore. Amelia Island
includes both the historic seaport of
Fernandina Beach with its lovingly restored
buildings and fabulous seafood, alongside
world-class beaches, golf, and tennis.

Northeast
Florida

Amelia Island

The first known inhabitants of Amelia Island were the Timucuan Indians. At the time of the arrival of the French explorer Jean Ribault in 1562, there were more than 20,000 Timucuans in Northern Florida. A Santa Maria mission was established on the island by Pedro Menendez in 1567, just two years after his discovery of the city of St. Augustine, sixty miles to the south. For more than 100 years, the Catholic priests lived and worked among the native Timucuans and were responsible for spreading Christianity and the written word throughout the island.

Amelia Island Williams House Grapefruit Special

1 *Florida grapefruit*
Butter
Dark brown sugar
1 *slice of kiwifruit*
1 *strawberry*

Remove the top ⅓ to ½ of the grapefruit. Section the remaining grapefruit. Place a pat of butter ⅛ to ¼ inch thick in the center of the grapefruit. Place about ¼ inch of dark brown sugar on top of the butter. Line a baking sheet with aluminum foil. Place the grapefruit on the baking sheet. Preheat the broiler. Broil for 5 to 8 minutes or until the rind starts to get dark. Remove from the oven. Place the kiwifruit slice and the strawberry in the center of the grapefruit. Place the individual grapefruit in a grapefruit dish. Place the grapefruit dish on a serving platter. Garnish with fresh flowers from the garden, arranging an additional slice of kiwifruit, an additional fresh strawberry and a banana half next to the flower. This makes a beautiful presentation and is delicious.

Yield: 1 serving

Amelia Island Williams House Eggs Benedict

4 English muffins,
    split and toasted
16 slices Canadian bacon
8 eggs
¼ cup butter
¼ cup flour
1 teaspoon paprika
⅛ teaspoon nutmeg
⅛ teaspoon pepper
2 cups milk
2 cups shredded Swiss cheese
½ cup dry white wine

Arrange the muffins cut side up in a 9x13-inch baking dish. Place 2 bacon slices on each muffin half. Fill a 10-inch skillet half full with water. Bring just to a boil. Break 1 egg into a dish; do not break the yolk. Slide the egg into the boiling water. Repeat with the remaining 7 eggs. Simmer, uncovered, until the eggs are just set. Remove the eggs 1 at a time with a slotted spoon and place on top of a muffin stack. Set aside. Melt ¼ cup butter in a medium saucepan. Whisk in the flour, paprika, nutmeg and pepper. Add the milk. Cook until thickened and bubbly, stirring constantly. Add the cheese. Cook until the cheese is melted, stirring constantly. Stir in the wine. Reserve enough sauce to cover each stack at serving time. Chill, covered, in the refrigerator. Spoon the remaining sauce over the muffin stacks. Chill, tightly covered, for 8 to 10 hours. Preheat the oven to 350 degrees. Bake, uncovered, for 20 to 25 minutes or until heated through. Heat the reserved sauce in a saucepan. Spoon over each stack. Garnish with a dash of parsley flakes and paprika.

Yield: 8 servings

The Amelia Island Williams House

Chris Carter and Dick Flitz
103 South Ninth Street
Amelia Island, Florida 32034
(904) 277-2328 or
(800) 414-9257

The Amelia Island Williams House received the "One of the Top 12 Inns of the Year 1995" award from Country Inns magazine. It was also voted "One of the Top 25 Inns of the South" by National Geographic Traveler. This 1856 antebellum mansion is filled with antiques from more than ten countries. The house has eight magnificent rooms, fireplaces, and Jacuzzis. Breakfast is served. Guests also enjoy a wine social hour.

Amelia Island

During English occupation of the island in 1702, James Oglethorpe, Governor of Georgia, renamed the island after Amelia, daughter of King George II. The seaport area of Fernandina, on the northwest corner of the island, was later named for Don Domingo Fernandez, a large landowner at the time.

Baked French Toast

1 *loaf French bread*
8 *ounces cream cheese, softened*
1 *cup blueberries or raspberries*
10 *eggs*
1 1/2 *cups half-and-half*
1/3 *cup maple syrup*
1/2 *cup melted butter*

Cut the bread into cubes. Spray a 9x13-inch baking dish with nonstick cooking spray. Place half the bread cubes in the prepared baking dish. Cut the cream cheese into small pieces. Scatter cream cheese pieces across the bread. Sprinkle blueberries over the cream cheese. Cover the blueberries with the remaining bread cubes. Combine the eggs, half-and-half, syrup and melted butter in a bowl and mix well. Pour the egg mixture over the bread cubes. Chill, covered, for 8 to 10 hours. Preheat the oven to 350 degrees. Bake, uncovered, for 40 to 50 minutes or until set.

Yield: 15 *servings*

Poppy Seed Muffins

2 cups flour
¼ cup poppy seeds
½ teaspoon salt
¼ teaspoon baking soda
½ cup butter, softened
¾ cup sugar
2 eggs
¾ cup sour cream
½ teaspoon vanilla extract

Preheat the oven to 375 degrees. Combine the flour, poppy seeds, salt and baking soda in a bowl and mix well. Set aside. Cream the butter and sugar in a mixer bowl until light and fluffy. Add the eggs 1 at a time, mixing well after each addition. Add the sour cream and vanilla and mix well. Add the dry ingredients gradually, beating well after each addition. Fill 12 greased 2-inch-diameter muffin cups ⅔ full. Bake for 20 minutes.

Yield: 12 *muffins*

The Bailey House
Tom and Jenny Bishop
28 South 7th Street
Amelia Island, Florida 32034
(904) 261-5390 or
(800) 251-5390

The Bailey House, built in 1895 and on the National Historic Register, is a Queen Anne-style home, located in the Historic District of Fernandina Beach, Florida. Nine spacious rooms, furnished with antiques, have the added comfort of individual bathrooms and air conditioning. Pets and smoking are not allowed in the house. Children over 8 years old are welcome. An extended full breakfast is served. MasterCard, VISA, and American Express credit cards are accepted.

Amelia Island

For more than 200 years, Amelia Island's harbor was a frequent stop for pirates and buccaneers. As a part of Spanish territory and not subject to U.S. patrol, the port of Fernandina became one of the pirate's busiest centers in the Western Hemisphere. Rumors of gold and buried treasure remain to this day.

Uncle Frank's Pastry Puffs

3 cups flour, sifted
1 tablespoon baking powder
½ teaspoon ground nutmeg
1 teaspoon salt
2 cups sugar
¾ cup shortening
2 eggs
1 cup milk
1 teaspoon ground cinnamon
¼ cup melted butter

Preheat the oven to 350 degrees. Combine the flour, baking powder, nutmeg and salt in a large bowl and mix well. Cream 1 cup of the sugar and the shortening in a bowl until light and fluffy. Add the eggs and mix well. Add the milk to the dry ingredients and blend thoroughly. Add to the creamed mixture and blend thoroughly. Spray 24 miniature muffin cups with nonstick cooking spray. Spoon the batter into the prepared muffin cups. Bake for 20 minutes. Cool in the muffin cups for 10 minutes. Remove to a wire rack to cool completely. Combine the remaining 1 cup sugar and cinnamon in a small bowl and mix well. Dip each muffin in the melted butter and then into the cinnamon-sugar mixture.

Note: Reduce the oven temperature to 325 degrees to bake in a convection oven.

Yield: 24 muffins

Miss Ona's Orange Juice Bread

½ cup unsalted butter

1¼ cups sugar

2 eggs, beaten

1½ cups all-purpose or
    unbleached flour

1 teaspoon baking powder

¼ teaspoon salt

¼ cup orange juice

¼ cup milk

Grated zest of 1 lemon

Grated zest of 1 orange

Citrus Juice Icing (below)

Preheat the oven to 325 degrees. Cream the butter and sugar in a bowl until light and fluffy. Add the eggs and mix well. Sift the flour, baking powder and salt together. Combine the orange juice and milk in a small bowl and mix well. Add the sifted dry ingredients and milk mixture alternately to the creamed mixture, mixing well after each addition. Stir in the lemon and orange zest. Butter a 5x9-inch loaf pan. Line the bottom of the pan with waxed paper. Butter the waxed paper. Pour the batter into the prepared pan. Bake for 45 minutes or until the loaf springs back when lightly touched in the center. Remove the loaf from the pan. Cool for 15 minutes on side. Remove the waxed paper. Drizzle the top of the loaf with Citrus Juice Icing.

Yield: 1 loaf

Citrus Juice Icing

1 tablespoon lemon juice

1 tablespoon orange juice

⅓ cup confectioners' sugar

Combine the lemon juice, orange juice and confectioners' sugar in a small bowl and mix well.

Yield: ⅓ cup

Elizabeth Pointe Lodge

David and Susan Caples
98 South Fletcher Avenue
Amelia Island, Florida 32034
(904) 277-4851 or
(800) 772-3359

The Elizabeth Pointe Lodge is rated "One of the Twelve Best Waterfront Inns" in America. The main house is constructed in an 1890s "Nantucket shingle"-style with a strong maritime theme. Sitting prominently on the Atlantic Ocean, the inn is only steps from often-deserted beaches. The inn contains twenty-five guest rooms/suites with private baths. A complimentary breakfast is served to guests. Other amenities include a daily newspaper and fresh flowers. Horseback riding, tennis, golf, and sailing are located nearby.

Amelia Island

The modern shrimping industry was born in Fernandina in the early 1900s, when local captains began taking powerboats into deeper waters. They made numerous refinements to the design of their trawl nets. As time went on, shrimp boats were able to travel further out to sea to pursue a wider variety of shrimp.

Amaretto Applesauce

1 *cup golden raisins*
2 *cups chunky applesauce*
1 *cup crushed pineapple, drained*
1/4 *cup packed brown sugar*
1 *teaspoon cinnamon*
1/4 *cup amaretto*

Place the raisins in a saucepan. Add water to cover. Bring to a boil. Boil for 5 minutes. Remove from heat. Let stand for 8 to 10 hours. Drain the raisins. Combine the raisins, applesauce, pineapple, brown sugar, cinnamon and amaretto in a saucepan and mix well. Cook over low heat until the sugar dissolves, stirring occasionally. Serve warm.

Yield: 8 servings

Baked Tomato French Toast

16 *slices wheat or multi-grain*
   bread
2 *tablespoons melted butter*
12 *slices Canadian bacon*
2 *cups shredded Cheddar cheese*
8 *eggs*
3 *cups half-and-half*
1 *teaspoon salt*
¼ *teaspoon pepper*
3 *tomatoes, cored, sliced*
2 *tablespoons chopped fresh basil*

Preheat the oven to 350 degrees. Place the bread in a single layer in a 10x15-inch baking dish. Brush lightly with the melted butter. Turn the bread butter side down in the dish. Arrange the Canadian bacon over the bread. Sprinkle 1¾ cups of the cheese over the Canadian bacon. Combine the eggs, half-and-half, salt and pepper in a bowl and mix well. Pour the egg mixture over the cheese. Bake, uncovered, for 15 minutes or until almost firm. Arrange the tomatoes over the top. Bake for 8 minutes. Sprinkle with the remaining ¼ cup cheese. Sprinkle with fresh basil.

Yield: *12 servings*

The Fairbanks House

Bill and Theresa Hamilton
227 South Seventh Street
Amelia Island, Florida 32034
(904) 277-0500 or
(800) 261-4838

Enjoy a bygone era in this National Historic Register nineteenth century Italianate villa, located in historic Fernandina Beach. Delight in the grandeur of the inn's arched piazzas, courtyard, swimming pool, and enchanted gardens. Guests will encounter splendor and comfort in each of the twelve guest rooms, suites, or cottages furnished with four-poster beds, Jacuzzis, claw-foot tubs, and fireplaces.

Throughout its colorful history, eight flags have flown over Amelia Island—French, Spanish, English, Patriots of Amelia Island, Green Cross of Florida, Mexican Rebel Flag, United States, and Confederate. Today, all eight flags hang in front of the Florida House Inn—stop by for the story, along with a "boarding house"-style lunch of Southern cooking.

Stuffed Yellow Squash

1 (10-ounce) package frozen chopped spinach, thawed
6 medium to large yellow squash
1 bay leaf, bruised
1 medium yellow onion, minced
2 cloves of garlic, crushed
½ cup melted butter
1 small can chopped anchovy fillets (optional)
1 cup sour cream
Dash of hot sauce to taste
Grated Parmesan cheese to taste
Seasoned bread crumbs to taste

Drain the thawed spinach, squeezing out as much moisture as possible. Cut the squash into halves lengthwise. Scoop out and discard the seedy pulp, leaving a ¼-inch-thick shell. Steam the squash with the bay leaf just until tender-crisp. Drain the squash, discarding the bay leaf. Let stand cut side down to cool. Sauté the onion and garlic in 2 tablespoons of the butter in a skillet. Add the spinach, anchovies, sour cream and hot sauce. Cook over medium heat for 10 to 15 minutes or until thickened, stirring constantly. Preheat the oven to 350 degrees. Arrange the squash cut side up in a buttered shallow baking dish. Spoon the spinach mixture into the squash shells. Sprinkle the spinach mixture with Parmesan cheese and bread crumbs, pressing crumbs gently into the spinach mixture. Drizzle with the remaining melted butter. Bake for 15 minutes or until bubbly. Broil for 1 minute to brown.

Yield: 12 servings

Selmarie's Sunday Cake

This wonderful, easy cake is a hit for any meal, dessert, breakfast, or midday tea party. We make this every Sunday for part of our breakfast offering, and it is always devoured!

2 cups flour

1 teaspoon baking powder

½ teaspoon baking soda

½ teaspoon salt

1 cup butter or margarine,
    softened

1¼ cups sugar

2 eggs

1 teaspoon vanilla extract

1 cup sour cream

3 tablespoons sugar

1½ teaspoons cinnamon

Preheat the oven to 350 degrees. Grease and flour a 10-inch fluted tube pan or bundt pan. Combine the flour, baking powder, baking soda and salt in a bowl and mix well. Cream the butter and 1¼ cups sugar in a mixer bowl until light and fluffy. Add the eggs and vanilla and mix well. Add the dry ingredients and sour cream alternately to the creamed mixture, mixing well after each addition. Pour half the batter into the prepared pan. Combine 3 tablespoons sugar and cinnamon in a bowl and mix well. Sprinkle over the batter in the pan. Pour the remaining batter over the cinnamon-sugar. Bake for 45 to 50 minutes or until a wooden pick inserted near the center comes out clean. Cool in the pan for 15 minutes. Invert onto a wire rack to cool completely. Sprinkle with sifted confectioners' sugar.

Yields: 14 to 16 servings

Florida House Inn

Bob and Karen Warner
20 & 22 South Third Street
Amelia Island, Florida 32034
(904) 261-3300 or
(800) 258-3301

There is a place tucked away in the northeast corner of Florida that is like no other. It is called the Florida House Inn, the oldest, continually operating inn in the state. Come and let our history come alive for you amid porch rockers, quilts, antiques, and live oaks. On the National Historic Register, the Florida House Inn features a cozy pub; a boarding house-style restaurant, which serves a full breakfast; and a shaded courtyard with gazebo and fountain. The inn's fifteen rooms feature fireplaces and Jacuzzi tubs.

Amelia Island

Construction of Fort Clinch, now a Florida State Park, was originally begun in the mid-1800s. The partially completed fort was seized by the Confederate Army at the beginning of the Civil War. Later on, Union troops regained control and attempted to continue construction of it until 1867, when it was stopped permanently.

Fruited-Stuffed Chicken Breasts

3 tablespoons minced shallots
¼ cup chopped dried apricots
¼ cup chopped dried cherries, cranberries or golden raisins
2 tablespoons coarsely chopped walnuts
1 cup soft bread crumbs
3 tablespoons butter
Salt and pepper to taste
¼ cup chardonnay or chicken broth
4 large boneless skinless chicken breasts
Spinach leaves
Chardonnay Ginger Sauce (below)

Preheat the oven to 400 degrees. Sauté the shallots, apricots, cherries, walnuts and bread crumbs in 2 tablespoons of the butter in a skillet until the bread crumbs brown slightly. Season with salt and pepper. Add the chardonnay and mix well. Pound the chicken breasts until thin. Sprinkle with salt and pepper. Rinse the spinach leaves and pat dry. Discard the stems. Top each chicken breast with the spinach leaves and fruit stuffing. Roll as for a jelly roll from the long side to form a tight roll. Secure with wooden picks or string. Melt the remaining 1 tablespoon of butter in an ovenproof skillet. Brown the chicken rolls on all sides in the skillet. Bake for 10 to 15 minutes or until cooked through. Remove wooden picks or string. Slice the chicken rolls into pinwheels. Fan on a serving plate. Serve with Chardonnay Ginger Sauce.

Yield: 4 servings

Chardonnay Ginger Sauce

2 tablespoons minced shallots
2 teaspoons grated gingerroot
⅓ cup chardonnay
1 cup cream
Salt to taste
1 teaspoon minced mint

Combine the shallots, gingerroot and chardonnay in a saucepan. Bring to a boil. Boil until reduced by half. Add the cream. Cook until of the desired consistency, stirring occasionally. Stir in the salt and mint.

Yield: 1 cup

Almond Skillet Coffee Cake

¾ *cup melted butter*
1¾ *cups sugar*
2 *eggs*
1½ *cups flour*
Pinch of salt
1 *teaspoon almond extract*
½ *cup slivered almonds*

Preheat the oven to 350 degrees. Combine the butter and 1½ cups of the sugar in a bowl and mix well. Add the eggs 1 at a time, mixing well after each addition. Add the flour, salt and almond extract and mix well. Line a cast-iron skillet with aluminum foil extending over the side. Pour the batter into the prepared skillet. Sprinkle the almonds and the remaining ¼ cup sugar on top. Bake for 30 to 35 minutes or until the coffee cake tests done. Cool completely before serving.

Yield: 12 *servings*

Hoyt House

John and Rita Kovacevich
804 Atlantic Avenue
Amelia Island, Florida 32034
(904) 277-4300 or
(800) 432-2085

The beauty and grace of this 1905 Queen Anne residence overflows with warmth, charm, and unparalleled service. The refined, yet relaxed, environment, combined with the nine unique bedchambers with private baths, will embrace and welcome all who enter. Linger over our sumptuous gourmet breakfast. Enjoy fireplaces, antiques, collectibles, porch, gazebo, garden, giraffes, and hot tub. Hoyt House features special-value romantic getaway, golf, and extended-stay packages.

Amelia Island

A fifty-three block area of Fernandina is listed as a Historic District on the National Register and is reminiscent of the days when this city was a thriving Victorian seaport. A magnificent collection of architectural styles, dominated by late Victorian but also including Italianate, Greek Revival, Neoclassical, and Colonial Revival, line the quiet, tree-lined streets.

Coconut Coffee Cake

1 (2-layer) package yellow
    cake mix
1 (4-ounce) package toasted
    coconut pudding mix
4 eggs
1 cup sour cream
½ cup vegetable oil
1 cup packed brown sugar
1 teaspoon cinnamon
½ cup chopped nuts

Preheat the oven to 350 degrees. Combine the cake mix, pudding mix and eggs in a mixer bowl and beat for 2 minutes or until smooth. Add the sour cream and oil and beat for 2 minutes or until smooth. Pour into a greased bundt pan. Combine the brown sugar, cinnamon and chopped nuts in a small bowl and mix well. Sprinkle the nut mixture over the batter. Cut through the cake batter and topping with a knife to marbleize. Bake for 1 hour or until the cake tests done. Cool in the pan for 10 minutes. Invert onto a serving plate and serve.

Yield: 16 servings

Apple French Toast

1 *cup packed brown sugar*
½ *cup butter*
2 *tablespoons light corn syrup*
2 *large tart apples, peeled, sliced*
3 *eggs*
1 *cup milk*
1 *teaspoon vanilla extract*
9 *(¾-inch-thick) slices day-old*
   French bread
1 *cup applesauce*
1 *(10-ounce) jar apple jelly*
½ *teaspoon cinnamon*

Combine the brown sugar, butter and corn syrup in a saucepan. Cook for 5 minutes or until thickened, stirring occasionally. Pour into a 9x13-inch baking pan. Arrange the apples on top. Combine the eggs, milk and vanilla in a bowl and mix well. Soak the bread slices in the egg mixture for 1 minute. Place the bread slices over the apples. Refrigerate, covered, for 8 to 10 hours. Remove from the refrigerator 30 minutes before baking. Preheat the oven to 350 degrees. Bake, uncovered, for 35 to 40 minutes or until set. Combine the applesauce, apple jelly and cinnamon in a saucepan. Cook until heated through, stirring constantly. Spoon over the French toast. Serve with whipped cream, if desired.

Yield: 9 servings

The Walnford Inn Bed & Breakfast

Bob and Linda Waln
102 South Seventh Street
Amelia Island, Florida 32034
(904) 277-4941 or
(800) 277-6660

The Walnford Inn and Guest House is a gracious turn-of-the-century home, located in the middle of beautiful historic Fernandina Beach, one block from downtown Centre Street. The Walnford Inn welcomes its guests with real southern hospitality. Each of its nine beautifully appointed rooms features its own personality and private bath.

Jacksonville

Within the Historic District of Riverside, southwest of downtown Jacksonville on the west side of the St. Johns River, is the St. Johns Quarter with a concentration of Prairie-style architecture not found anywhere else in the South. The Prairie style has its roots in the Midwest and was developed by young architects, following the influence of Frank Lloyd Wright. Most of these houses, like the Cleary-Dickert House, are two stories with gabled or hipped roofs, frequently bisected by dormers. Most of these homes feature front porches and formal areas.

Strawberry Muffins

1 ¼ cups flour
2 ½ teaspoons baking powder
½ teaspoon salt
1 cup rolled oats
½ cup sugar
1 cup milk
½ cup melted butter or margarine
1 egg, beaten
1 teaspoon vanilla extract
1 cup chopped strawberries

Preheat the oven to 425 degrees. Sift the flour, baking powder and salt into a large bowl. Add the rolled oats and sugar and mix well. Combine the milk, butter, egg and vanilla in a small bowl and mix well. Stir the milk mixture into the dry ingredients just until moistened. Stir in the strawberries. Spoon the batter into 12 greased 2½-inch muffin cups, filling each ⅔ full. Bake for 15 to 18 minutes or until lightly browned and a wooden pick inserted into the centers comes out clean.

Yield: 12 muffins

Strawberry and Banana-Stuffed French Toast

1 loaf French bread
2 tablespoons strawberry jam
4 ounces cream cheese, softened
¼ cup chopped strawberries
¼ cup chopped banana
6 eggs, lightly beaten
¾ cup milk
3 tablespoons butter or margarine
Strawberry Sauce (below)

Cut the French bread into eight 1½-inch slices. Make a pocket in each slice by cutting a slit from the top of the bread almost to the bottom. Combine the jam, cream cheese, strawberries and banana in a small bowl and blend thoroughly. Place a heaping tablespoonful of strawberry filling into each pocket. Press back together. Combine the eggs and milk in a wide shallow bowl and mix well. Add the bread. Let stand to coat; turn the bread over to coat the other side. Melt 2 tablespoons of the butter in a large skillet over medium-low heat. Add as many bread slices as will fit. Cook until brown on both sides, turning once. Remove and keep warm. Repeat with the remaining 1 tablespoon of butter and bread slices. Serve with Strawberry Sauce.

Yield: 8 servings

Strawberry Sauce

1 pint strawberries, hulled
2 to 3 teaspoons sugar
1 tablespoon strawberry- or
   orange-flavored liqueur

Combine the strawberries, sugar and liqueur in a blender container and process until smooth.

Yield: 1½ cups

Cleary-Dickert House

Joe Cleary and Betty Dickert
1804 Copeland Street
Jacksonville, Florida 32204
(904) 387-4762

The Cleary-Dickert House is located fifty yards from the river in historical Riverside. It is located ten minutes from downtown and five minutes from Interstates 10 and 95. Combining English tradition with Southern hospitality, the English gardens lead guests to the elegant 1914 home, which features three luxurious guest suites with private baths, sitting rooms, and bedrooms. Complete gourmet breakfast and afternoon tea or cocktails are served.

Jacksonville

The Riverside Historic District, on the National Register of Historic Places, began when 500 acres of land, known as Dell's Bluff, was purchased by newspaper editor Edward Cheney in 1868. Cheney was acting as an agent for John Murray Forbes, a Boston millionaire who subdivided the land and named it Riverside. Prominent citizens slowly moved into the area and built homes, but it was not until the Great Fire of 1901 that development in the area took off. It became home to an assortment of prominent and colorful citizens. Frank Slaughter wrote thirty of his books while living in the area, descendants of the founder of Maxwell House built a replica of an English castle, and even today Riverside is one of the largest Historic Districts in Florida.

Heart-Healthy Soufflé in Ramekins

6 eggs, or an equivalent amount
    of egg substitute
¼ cup melted butter
½ teaspoon baking soda
1 cup cottage cheese
8 ounces Cheddar cheese,
    shredded
Salt and pepper to taste

Preheat the oven to 400 degrees. Combine the eggs, butter, baking soda, cottage cheese, Cheddar cheese, salt and pepper in a bowl and mix well. Pour into 6 ramekins sprayed with non-stick cooking spray, filling ⅔ full. Bake for 20 to 25 minutes or until a wooden pick inserted in the center comes out clean.

Note: A meat or vegetable can be added for color or texture.

Yield: 6 servings

Cherry Street Cheesy Breakfast

1 ½ cups frozen loose-pack hash
  brown potatoes, thawed
1 cup shredded Monterey Jack
  cheese with jalapeños
1 cup shredded Swiss cheese
1 cup chopped cooked ham or
  Canadian bacon
1 (4-ounce) can mushrooms
4 eggs, well beaten
1 cup half-and-half
½ cup sour cream

Preheat the oven to 450 degrees. Drain and press the potatoes to remove excess moisture. Arrange potatoes in a greased 8- or 9-inch square baking pan. Bake for 20 minutes. Cool for 10 minutes. Reduce the oven temperature to 350 degrees. Sprinkle the Monterey Jack cheese, Swiss cheese, chopped ham and mushrooms over the potatoes. Combine the eggs, half-and-half and sour cream in a bowl and mix well. Pour over the layers. Bake for 25 minutes. Let stand for 5 minutes before serving.

Yield: 6 servings

House on Cherry Street

Carol Anderson
1844 Cherry Street
Jacksonville, Florida 32205
(904) 384-1999

House on Cherry Street is an award-winning, restored colonial home on beautiful St. Johns River in historic Riverside. It is located ten minutes from downtown and twenty minutes from the airport. Enjoy fresh flowers, period antique canopy beds, decoys, baskets, coverlets, and other collectibles in each of the four air-conditioned rooms. Amenities include continental breakfast, complimentary wine, and hors d'oeuvres.

St. Augustine

St. Augustine was founded on September 8, 1565 by Pedro Menendez de Aviles for King Philip II of Spain. Through the trials of war, starvation, and devastating storms, it has existed through more than 430 years and has spanned a longer chronicle of history than any other city in the United States.

Butter Chocolate Brownies

2 cups sugar
6 tablespoons baking cocoa
1 cup butter, softened
2 teaspoons vanilla extract
1 cup flour
4 eggs
1 cup chopped nuts

Preheat the oven to 350 degrees. Combine the sugar, baking cocoa, butter and vanilla in a mixer bowl and mix well. Add the flour and eggs alternately, mixing well after each addition. Stir in the nuts. Pour the brownie batter into a greased and floured 9x13-inch baking pan. Bake for 45 minutes or until brownies begin to pull away from the sides of the pan.

Yield: 24 brownies

Carriage Way Quiche

1 unbaked (9-inch) pie shell
2 eggs, beaten
2 cups half-and-half
½ cup shredded sharp
   Cheddar cheese
1 tablespoon melted butter
¼ teaspoon salt
¼ teaspoon white pepper
5 slices bacon, minced
½ cup chopped onion
½ cup minced cooked ham
½ cup shredded Swiss cheese

Preheat the oven to 400 degrees. Prick bottom of pie shell with a fork several times. Bake for 8 minutes. Remove the pie shell from the oven. Reduce the oven temperature to 350 degrees. Combine the eggs, half-and-half, Cheddar cheese, butter, salt and white pepper in a bowl and mix well. Set aside. Fry the bacon in a skillet until crisp. Drain the bacon, reserving a small amount of bacon drippings. Crumble the bacon into the partially baked pie shell. Sauté the onion in the reserved bacon drippings in a skillet until translucent. Add the ham. Cook until the ham is heated through. Spoon over the bacon. Sprinkle with the Swiss cheese. Pour the egg mixture over the layers. Bake for 25 to 30 minutes or until set.

Yield: 6 servings

**Carriage Way
Bed & Breakfast**

Bill and Diane Johnson
70 Cuna Street
St. Augustine, Florida 32084
(800) 908-9832

Carriage Way is an 1883 romantic Victorian bed-and-breakfast with nine rooms. Each room is furnished with antiques and reproductions, including brass and canopy beds. Amenities include breakfast, cordials, newspaper, and bicycles. Special touches include our "Sweetheart" packages for honeymoons, anniversaries, and other special days.

In the late seventeenth century,
following the establishment
of other Southeastern colonies, the
massive, stone fortress, Castillo
de San Marcos, was built in
hopes of protecting the Spanish
city from the sea and preserving
Spain's military position
in America.

Nina's Pineapple Upside-Down French Toast

6 eggs
¾ teaspoon salt
1 tablespoon sugar
1 tablespoon vanilla extract
⅛ teaspoon almond extract
2½ cups low-fat milk
2 tablespoons light brown sugar
6 slices canned pineapple
6 maraschino cherry halves
12 slices honey wheat bread

Preheat the oven to 350 degrees. Combine the eggs, salt, sugar, vanilla and almond extract in a bowl and mix well. Add the milk and blend thoroughly. Spray a 9x14-inch baking pan with nonstick cooking spray. Sprinkle the brown sugar over the bottom of the baking pan. Arrange the pineapple slices over the brown sugar. Place a cherry half round side down in each pineapple center. Place 1 bread slice on each pineapple slice. Pour half the milk mixture over the bread. Place the remaining slices of bread over the first layer of bread, forming 6 stacks. Pour the remaining milk mixture over the bread. Place the pan on a large baking sheet to prevent the bottom from burning. Bake for 45 minutes. Serve with maple syrup or thickened pineapple juice syrup.

Note: May be prepared the night before and baked in the morning.

Yield: 6 servings

Russ' Ruffled Eggs

6 slices honey wheat bread

6 eggs

Salt to taste

Pepper to taste

Garlic powder to taste

1 (10-ounce) can cream of
   chicken soup

5 ounces low-fat milk

½ (10-ounce) can yams or sweet
   potatoes, chopped

Hot sauce to taste

Cinnamon to taste

1 small tomato, seeded, chopped

1 tablespoon chopped green onions

Paprika to taste

Preheat the oven to 350 degrees. Spray a 6-cup Texas-size muffin pan with nonstick cooking spray. Press 1 slice of bread into each cup leaving a scalloped or ruffled edge sticking above the cup. Break 1 egg into each bread shell. Sprinkle salt, pepper and garlic powder on each egg. Bake for 18 minutes or until the eggs are set. Combine the soup and milk in a microwave-safe bowl and mix well. Add the yams, hot sauce and cinnamon and mix well. Microwave on High for 4 minutes. Remove egg cups from muffin cups and place on individual serving plates. Spoon the yam mixture over each egg cup. Top with tomato, green onions and paprika. Garnish with a slice of orange and a fresh strawberry.

Yield: 6 servings

Cedar House Inn

Russ and Nina Thomas
79 Cedar Street, East
St. Augustine, Florida 32084
(904) 829-0079 or
(800) 233-2746

Capture romantic moments at our 1893 Victorian home, located in the heart of the ancient city of St. Augustine. Escape into a Jacuzzi suite or antique-filled bedroom with claw-footed tub. Enjoy the Grand Parlour's fireplace and player piano. Elegant full breakfast, complimentary beverages, homemade cookies, convenient on-premise parking, outside Jacuzzi, and bicycles are all a part of the Cedar House Inn experience. Midweek special rates are available.

Dattil Pepper Strawberry Crepes

1¾ *cups flour*
1 *cup cold milk*
1 *cup cold water*
4 *eggs*
½ *cup melted butter*
Cream Cheese Filling (below)
Dattil Pepper Sauce (page 41)

Combine the flour, milk, water and eggs in
a bowl and mix well. Stir in the melted butter.
Refrigerate for 1 hour. Heat a small skillet.
Spoon ¼ cup of the batter into the skillet.
Lift and tilt the skillet to spread the batter.
Brown lightly on 1 side. Flip the crepe out of
the skillet and onto a sheet of waxed paper.
Repeat with the remaining batter, stacking
each crepe between waxed paper. Let stand
until cool. Preheat the oven to 350 degrees.
Fill crepes with Cream Cheese Filling. Roll
crepes to enclose the filling, sealing the edges.
Place on a baking sheet. Bake for 10 minutes.
Drizzle the Dattil Pepper Sauce on each plate.
Place 2 crepes on top. Garnish with fresh
strawberries and confectioners' sugar.

Yield: 8 servings

Cream Cheese Filling

12 *ounces cream cheese, softened*
¼ *cup sugar*
2 *tablespoons lemon juice*

Combine the cream cheese, sugar and
lemon juice in a mixer bowl and beat until
light and fluffy.

Yield: 1½ cups

Dattil Pepper Sauce

1 jar Dattil pepper strawberry
    preserves
1 cup light corn syrup

Combine the Dattil pepper strawberry preserves and corn syrup in a saucepan and mix thoroughly. Cook until heated through.

Yield: 2 cups

Baked Egg Fluff

1 cup chopped green bell pepper
12 ounces mushrooms, sliced
8 to 10 slices of bread, crusts
    trimmed, cubed
½ cup melted butter
1¼ cups shredded Monterey Jack,
    Cheddar or Swiss cheese
8 ounces bacon or ham bits
8 to 10 egg yolks
2 cups milk
¼ teaspoon salt
⅛ teaspoon pepper
8 to 10 egg whites

Sauté the green pepper and mushrooms in a small amount of butter in a skillet. Place enough bread cubes in a greased 9x13-inch baking pan to cover the bottom. Pour the melted butter over the bread cubes. Sprinkle the sautéed green peppers and mushrooms, cheese and bacon bits over the bread cubes. Combine the egg yolks, milk, salt and pepper in a bowl and mix well. Pour over the layers. Beat the egg whites at high speed in a mixer bowl until stiff peaks form. Spread over the top, sealing to the edges. Refrigerate, covered, for 8 to 10 hours. Preheat the oven to 325 degrees. Bake for 40 to 45 minutes or until cooked through.

Yield: 10 servings

The Old Powder House Inn B&B

Al and Eunice Howes
38 Cordova Street
St. Augustine, Florida 32084
(904) 824-4149 or
(800) 447-4149

Towering pecan and oak trees shade verandas with rockers, where you can watch the passing horses and buggies: an introduction to a romantic escape in this charming turn-of-the-century Victorian inn, located in the heart of the Historic District. Amenities include full gourmet breakfast, wine and hors d'oeuvres, Jacuzzi, TV, private baths, parking, and bicycles. Wedding and special packages are available.

St. Augustine

After spending his own honeymoon in this Southern city, Henry M. Flagler, self-made millionaire and founder of Standard Oil, decided that St. Augustine would become a winter resort for the northern rich. By financing the economic development of this city, he created an empire of hotels and railroads that reach from St. Augustine to Key West.

Peanut Butter Balls or "Buckeyes"

1 (1-pound) package
 confectioners' sugar
½ cup butter, softened
3½ cups crisp rice cereal
2 cups peanut butter
½ stick paraffin
1 pound semisweet
 chocolate chips

Combine the confectioners' sugar, butter, cereal and peanut butter in a bowl and mix well. Roll into 1-inch balls. Refrigerate until firm. Melt the paraffin and chocolate chips in a saucepan, stirring frequently. Dip the peanut butter balls into the chocolate using a wooden pick. Place on waxed paper. Let stand until cool. Store, covered, in the refrigerator.

Yield: 8 dozen balls

Smoked Sausage Bake

1 pound smoked sausage, sliced

1 cup mushrooms

6 slices bread, cubed

2 cups milk

6 eggs

1 teaspoon dry mustard

½ teaspoon celery seeds

1 teaspoon oregano

12 ounces Cheddar cheese,
   shredded

Sauté the sausage and mushrooms in a skillet until the sausage is cooked through; drain. Place the bread cubes in a greased 8x12-inch baking pan. Place the sausage mixture evenly over the bread. Combine the milk, eggs, mustard, celery seeds, oregano and Cheddar cheese in a bowl and mix well. Pour over the layers. Refrigerate, covered, for 8 to 10 hours. Preheat the oven to 350 degrees. Bake, uncovered, for 45 minutes or until set.

Yield: 10 to 12 servings

St. Francis Inn

Joe and Margaret Finnegan
279 St. George Street
St. Augustine, Florida 32084
(904) 824-6068 or
(800) 824-6062

Built in 1791, the St. Francis Inn
is a beautiful Spanish Colonial
building. The courtyard garden
provides a peaceful setting
for traditional hospitality.
Accommodations range from double
rooms and suites to a five-room
cottage—all with private baths, cable
TV, central air conditioning, and
phones. Many have fireplaces and
whirlpool tubs. The inn is centrally
located in the Historic District within
easy walking distance to restaurants,
shops, and historic sites. Fourteen
rooms are available. Conference
facilities are also offered.

Rural North Central Florida

Quiet lazy days surrounded by untapped beauty, or the perfect escape for outdoor recreation. Natural springs and large, crystal-clear rivers traverse this region, lined with live oaks and pines. Swimming, canoeing, and tubing is offered at each bend in the quiet road. Snorkel face to face with a gentle manatee, dive amongst the many natural springs. Wildlife can be found in nature, or at outstanding family-oriented attractions. Quiet towns are lined with antique shops, bookstores, and outdoor cafés. To locals and enthusiastic visitors, this is the real Florida.

North Central Florida

High Springs

Located in Alachua County, High Springs boasts some of the United States' most beautiful springs—Ginnie Springs, Poe Springs, and Blue Springs. Each year thousands of visitors spend quiet summer afternoons scuba diving and snorkeling in these springs, tubing down the Ichetucknee River, or canoeing or kayaking the Santa Fe and Suwannee Rivers. High Springs expanded rapidly as an important railroad center in the 1890s, and the magnificent homes of that era have helped to place this peaceful country town on the National Register of Historic Places.

Buttermilk Breakfast Biscuits

2½ *cups flour*
2 *tablespoons sugar*
1½ *teaspoons cream of tartar*
¾ *teaspoon baking soda*
½ *teaspoon salt*
½ *cup butter*
⅔ *cup buttermilk*
1 *egg*
Milk
Sugar

Preheat the oven to 425 degrees. Combine the flour, 2 tablespoons sugar, cream of tartar, baking soda and salt in a large bowl and mix well. Cut in the butter until the mixture resembles coarse meal. Stir in the buttermilk and egg. Turn dough out onto a floured surface and knead until smooth; dough will be moist. Roll dough out into a circle ½ inch thick. Place on a greased baking sheet. Cut into wedges. Brush top with milk. Sprinkle with sugar. Bake for 15 minutes or until golden brown.

Yield: 8 *to* 10 *servings*

Banana Muffins

6 tablespoons milk

2 teaspoons vinegar

¾ cup margarine, softened

2¼ cups sugar

3 eggs

1½ cups mashed bananas

3 cups flour

1½ teaspoons baking soda

1½ cups chopped pecans or
slivered almonds (optional)

Preheat the oven to 350 degrees. Mix the milk and vinegar in a small bowl. Cream the margarine and sugar in a bowl until light and fluffy. Add the eggs, bananas and milk mixture and mix well. Mix the flour and baking soda together. Add to the banana mixture and blend thoroughly. Pour the batter into muffin cups sprayed with nonstick cooking spray, filling each ⅔ full. Sprinkle a small amount of chopped pecans on top of each muffin cup. Bake for 30 minutes or until a wooden pick inserted in the centers comes out clean.

Yield: 12 to 18 muffins

The Rustic Inn

Diana and Larry Zorovich

3105 South Main Street

High Springs, Florida 32643

(904) 454-1223

Indulge yourself in the solitude afforded by a six-room inn, located on ten acres of beautiful countryside. Each of the 450-square-foot rooms is a mini-getaway with a complete private bath, refrigerator, coffeemaker, and microwave. The inn is located 2.2 miles south of historic downtown High Springs in the heart of North Central Florida's springs, rivers, and horse country.

Cedar Key

Cedar Key hasn't always been the idyllic, sleepy waterfront community it is today. In the late 1800s, it was a major seaport with more than 2,000 hotel rooms and was the western terminus of the first Trans Florida Railway. Cedar Key's rough-and-tumble history is best depicted by the story of a gun duel in the early 1900s. A steamboat captain and his first mate each took a shot. The first mate, though younger than the captain, was a better marksman. He killed the captain instantly, but not before suffering a wound himself. As the captain lay dying, he made his final request, "to bury that *&%&* at my feet." And, that's exactly what the townspeople did—for proof check out the "T"-shaped graves in the local cemetery.

Cindy Wiley's Country Biscuits

4 cups flour
4 teaspoons baking powder
1/2 teaspoon baking soda
1 teaspoon salt
1/4 cup shortening
1/4 cup unsalted butter
2 cups (or more) buttermilk

Preheat the oven to 450 degrees. Combine the flour, baking powder, baking soda and salt in a large bowl and mix well. Cut in the shortening and butter until crumbly. Add the buttermilk 1 cup at a time, mixing well after each addition. Mixture will be very moist. Add additional buttermilk if dough is not moist enough. Place dough on a lightly floured surface. Pat gently into a circle 1/2 inch thick. Cut out with a biscuit cutter. Arrange biscuits with sides touching on a baking sheet. Bake for 10 minutes or until golden brown.

Yield: 16 biscuits

Cindy's Biscuits Déjà Vu

15 *day-old biscuits*
2 *cups (about) milk*
1 *cup half-and-half*
1 *(21-ounce) can apple or*
   cherry pie filling
1 *cup dried fruit*
½ *cup flour*
½ *cup sugar*
½ *cup butter, softened*
2 *tablespoons cinnamon*

Preheat the oven to 450 degrees. Cut the biscuits into halves. Place in a 9x13-inch glass baking dish. Pour the milk and half-and-half over the biscuits. Spread the pie filling over the biscuits. Sprinkle with dried fruit. Combine the flour, sugar and butter in a bowl and mix until crumbly. Sprinkle over the dried fruit. Bake for 20 to 25 minutes or until the liquid is almost absorbed and the topping is light brown. Sprinkle the cinnamon over the top.

Yield: 15 servings

Cedar Key
Bed & Breakfast
Bob and Lois Davenport
Corner of 3rd and F Streets
P.O. Box 700
Cedar Key, Florida 32625
(352) 543-9000 or
(800) 453-5051,
access code 51

Cedar Key Bed & Breakfast provides Victorian ambience in a small island community, nestled among the tiny keys of the Nature Coast. Experience old Florida and enjoy unique Cedar Key sunsets from our veranda. Seven rooms with private baths and comfortable beds, along with a full breakfast in a garden setting, await you in this forgotten village by the sea.

Ocala

Ocala, centrally located in the middle of the Florida peninsula, is the potato chip capital of the east coast. Golden Flake Snack Foods churns out more than 100,000 bags of potato chips each day. So, you ask yourself, how many crispy chips can you make from one plump potato? Take the free tour on Wednesday or Thursday each week to find out!

Three-Cheese-Stuffed French Toast

8 (2-inch-thick) slices
   French bread
4 ounces cream cheese, softened
¾ cup shredded mozzarella cheese
1 tablespoon ricotta cheese
3 tablespoons apricot jam
2 eggs
½ cup milk
1 cup cornflake crumbs
2 tablespoons butter or margarine
¼ cup melted butter
2 teaspoons ground ginger
2 tablespoons sugar
16 fresh peach slices
Sifted confectioners' sugar
1 (12-ounce) bottle apricot syrup

Split each bread slice by starting from 1 side and butterfly. Hollow out the bread with a fork, discarding the crumbs. Set the bread slices aside. Combine the cream cheese, mozzarella cheese, ricotta cheese and apricot jam in a bowl and mix well. Spoon about 2 tablespoons of the cheese mixture into each bread slice. Place the bread slices in a 9x13-inch baking dish. Refrigerate, covered, for 8 to 10 hours. Combine the eggs and milk in a shallow dish and mix well. Dip the bread in the egg mixture coating both sides. Dredge in cornflake crumbs coating both sides. Preheat the oven to 400 degrees. Melt 2 tablespoons butter in a large skillet over medium heat. Cook the bread on each side for 2 minutes or until golden brown. Place the bread in a lightly greased 9x13-inch baking dish. Bake for 15 minutes. Combine ¼ cup butter, ginger, sugar and peaches in a large skillet. Cook over medium heat for 3 minutes, stirring gently. Arrange the French toast on individual serving plates. Top each serving with the peach slices. Sprinkle with confectioners' sugar. Serve with warm apricot syrup.

Yield: 8 servings

Chicken Puff Pastry

1 (10-ounce) package puff
  pastry shells
2 tablespoons butter or
  vegetable oil
3 tablespoons flour
2 cups clear chicken stock
1½ cups chopped cooked chicken
½ cup button mushrooms,
  chopped
¼ cup pimentos
1 egg yolk, beaten
1 tablespoon basil
2 tablespoons fancy thyme
2 teaspoons cooking sherry
  (optional)
Slivered almonds

Prepare the puff pastry shells using the
package directions. Melt the butter in a skillet.
Blend in the flour. Add the chicken stock
gradually, stirring until smooth. Bring to a boil.
Stir in the chicken, mushrooms and pimentos.
Reduce the heat. Add the egg yolk and mix
well. This adds texture and color. Cook until
the sauce is of the desired consistency, stirring
constantly. Stir in the basil, fancy thyme and
cooking sherry. Place a baked puff pastry shell
on each warm serving plate. Spoon the chicken
mixture into each shell. Sprinkle with slivered
almonds. Garnish with parsley.

Yield: 6 servings

Seven Sisters Inn

Bonnie Morehardt and Ken Oden
820 Southeast Fort King Street
Ocala, Florida 34471
(352) 867-1170 or
(800) 250-3496

Seven Sisters Inn, "Florida's
Enchantress," was named "Inn of the
Month" by Country Inns
Magazine. The Inn has also been
featured in Southern Living,
Condé Nast Traveler, and
National Geographic. The 1888
Victorian mansion was also judged to
be "Florida's Best Restoration." Eight
rooms feature king- and queen-size
suites, fireplaces, canopy beds, private
baths, soaking tubs, and Jacuzzi.
Amenities include gourmet breakfast,
afternoon tea, murder mysteries, and
candlelight dinners. Visit Silver
Springs, horse farms, and museums.
Canoeing, hiking, horseback riding,
and antiquing are also available.

Lady Lake

Many famous people have passed through this rural area of North Central Florida, but two of the most well-known were Ma and Fred Barker. The Feds closed in on Ma and her son on the north shore of Lake Weir, where they were vacationing. Confirming their location through an informant, one of the most famous shootouts in FBI annals began. Tours of the home and a reenactment are held once each year. Bullets still remain in many of the walls, as virtually thousands of rounds were expended during the battle.

Real Scotch Shortbread

1 *cup butter, softened*
½ *cup plus 2 tablespoons sugar*
2½ *cups flour*

Combine the butter and sugar in a bowl and mix thoroughly. Add the flour and mix using your hands. Chill the dough completely. Preheat the oven to 300 degrees. Roll the dough ⅓ to ½ inch thick on a floured surface. Cut in fancy shapes. Place on a nonstick cookie sheet. Bake for 20 to 25 minutes. Cookies do not brown or change shape. Cool on a wire rack.

Yield: 2 dozen

Creamed Eggs

¼ cup butter
1 tablespoon flour
1 cup milk
Salt and pepper to taste
4 hard-cooked eggs
8 slices whole wheat bread, plain
    or toasted, buttered if desired

Melt the butter in a large skillet over medium heat. Add the flour. Cook until the flour is brown, stirring constantly. Stir in the milk, salt and pepper. Increase the heat to high. Cook until the sauce is of the desired consistency, stirring constantly. Peel and chop the eggs. Stir into the sauce gradually. Arrange 2 slices of bread on each serving plate. Spoon the creamed eggs over the bread. Garnish with parsley.

Yield: 4 servings

Shamrock Thistle & Crown

Brantley and Anne Overcash
12971 Southeast CR 42
Weirsdale, Florida 32195
(352) 821-1887 or
(800) 425-2763

Enjoy luxurious whirlpool suites, romance, and fireside chats in the countryside at Shamrock Thistle & Crown. "Run away from it all" to our three-story Victorian inn, built in 1887. Wake up to an elegant breakfast, featuring Irish crystal and fine china, enjoyed in our formal dining room or in your bedchamber. We are quietly tucked away, yet only eight minutes from dining and dancing at many themed restaurants, located on a scenic town square. Championship golf courses and jet skiing are nearby. Silver Springs, Juniper Springs, or Alexander Springs, natural springs for canoeing, hiking, and bird watching, are only 25 minutes away. Horseback riding through the Ocala National Forest can be arranged. Complimentary cookies and beverages are served.

Bushnell

A rural gem, just one hour
north of Tampa, Bushnell is
surrounded by the 113,000 acre
Withlacoochee State Forest,
making it a perfect spot for
hiking, canoeing, and horseback
riding. This sleepy town comes
alive, however, each Monday,
when the Webster Flea Market,
one of the nation's largest, opens.
The nearby Dade Battlefield
State Historic Site commemorates
the ambush and massacre
of Major Francis Dade and his
troops by Seminole Indians in
December, 1835.

Bean Sprout and Sauerkraut Salad

1 (16-ounce) can sauerkraut,
    drained well
2 cups bean sprouts, rinsed,
    drained
1/2 cup sliced celery
1/4 cup chopped onion
2 tablespoons finely chopped
    green bell pepper
1 (2-ounce) jar pimento,
    drained, chopped
1/2 cup sugar
1/2 cup vinegar
1/4 cup salad oil

Combine the sauerkraut, bean sprouts, celery, onion, green pepper and pimento in a large bowl and mix well. Combine the sugar, vinegar and salad oil in a microwave-safe bowl and mix well. Microwave on High until the mixture comes to a boil. Pour dressing over the vegetables. Toss the vegetables to coat. Refrigerate, covered, for 8 to 10 hours.

Yield: 6 to 8 servings

Bread Pudding

4 *cups bread pieces*

2 *cups milk, scalded*

¼ *cup butter or margarine*

½ *cup sugar*

2 *eggs, beaten*

¼ *teaspoon salt*

1 *teaspoon cinnamon*

½ *cup raisins (optional)*

½ *cup chopped pecans or walnuts*
      (optional)

Preheat the oven to 350 degrees. Place the bread pieces in a 9x13-inch baking dish. Mix the scalded milk and butter in a bowl until the butter melts. Cool slightly. Combine the milk mixture, sugar, eggs, salt, cinnamon, raisins and pecans in a bowl and mix well. Pour over the bread, thoroughly soaking the bread. Bake for 35 minutes.

Yield: 15 *servings*

**Cypress House
Bed & Breakfast Inn**

Jan Fessler

5175 Southwest 90th Boulevard

Bushnell, Florida 33513

(352) 568-0909 *or*

(888) 568-1666

Enjoy Florida of the old days—trees, meadow, sky, and lots of open space. The inn is a large, new cypress-log house, located near the center of four-square-miles of nature, but only two miles from an I-75 exit. Enjoy rocking on our wraparound veranda. The inn has five cheerfully decorated rooms (three with a private bath), a pool, and riding horses. Canoeing, bike riding, and hiking can be enjoyed in the Withlacoochee State Forest. Amenities include a buffet breakfast and evening dessert.

Exciting Central Florida

Nowhere in the world is there more excitement
than in this region of Florida-Orlando's theme
park attractions, racing events in Daytona, and
shuttles hurtling into space at Cape Canaveral
and the Kennedy Space Center. Interspersed
are gentle, protected beaches,
lush tropical gardens, and
wildlife refuges offering
alternatives for quieter days.
When the excitement becomes too
much, sleepy "Old Florida" towns
throughout the region are buffer
escapes to wide porches, rockers, and
times gone by.

Central
Florida

New Smyrna Beach

New Smyrna Beach was established as an English colony by Dr. Andrew Turnbull in 1768. Dr. Turnbull named the colony Smyrna in honor of his wife's birthplace, a place in Asia Minor. Old Fort Park contains the Turnbull ruins, overlooking the inlet entrance from the sea. The Sugar Mill ruins are the center of a small state park and are very beautiful in their decay.

Chicken Enchiladas

¼ *cup butter*
2 *tablespoons cornstarch*
8 *ounces sour cream*
1 *cup half-and-half*
Garlic salt to taste
4 to 5 *chicken breasts, cooked, cut into chunks*
1 (10-count) *package small flour tortillas, at room temperature*
¼ *cup diced jalapeños*
½ *cup shredded mozzarella cheese*

Preheat the oven to 350 degrees. Melt the butter in a saucepan. Stir in the cornstarch until smooth. Add the sour cream and half-and-half and mix well. Bring to a boil, stirring occasionally. Reduce the heat. Simmer for 4 to 5 minutes or until thickened, stirring constantly. Sprinkle with garlic salt. Cover the bottom of an 8x13-inch baking pan with a thin layer of the sauce. Place the chicken chunks in the center of each tortilla. Spoon 2 tablespoons of the sauce over the chicken. Roll up the tortillas to enclose the filling. Place seam side down in the prepared pan. Cover with the remaining sauce. Bake, covered, with foil, for 20 minutes. Sprinkle jalapeños and mozzarella cheese over the top. Bake, uncovered, for 10 to 15 minutes or until brown and bubbly.

Yield: 6 to 8 servings

Tomato Pie

1 (9-inch) unbaked pie shell
4 to 6 ripe fresh tomatoes
¼ cup chopped chives or scallions
¾ teaspoon fresh basil, or
   ¼ teaspoon dried basil
¼ teaspoon salt
¼ teaspoon pepper
1 cup mayonnaise
1 cup shredded Monterey Jack
   cheese

Preheat the oven to 425 degrees. Prick the pie shell with a fork several times. Bake for 5 minutes. Reduce the oven temperature to 400 degrees. Rinse and slice the tomatoes. Layer the tomatoes in the pie shell, sprinkling chives, basil, salt and pepper between each layer and on top. Combine the mayonnaise and cheese in a bowl and mix well. Spread evenly over the tomatoes sealing to the edge of the pie shell. Bake for 35 minutes or until the pie is golden brown and bubbly. Let stand for 5 to 10 minutes before cutting.

Yield: 8 servings

Little River Inn

Joyce, Doug, and Wendy MacLean
532 North Riverside Drive
New Smyrna Beach, Florida 32168
(904) 424-0100 or
(888) 424-0102

Casual elegance and gracious Southern living combine when you visit our 1883 estate home. A meandering river brings blue herons and manatees to our doorstep. Wide expanses of lawn and nearly two acres of canopied oaks coax you into letting time go by. Come relax, swim, or surf in the nearby Atlantic Ocean. Browse in antique shops or just enjoy the rockers on our wide brick verandas.

Oven-Baked French Toast

2 *eggs, or an equivalent amount of egg substitute*
¼ *cup skim milk*
¼ *teaspoon cinnamon*
Dash of salt
6 *slices day-old French bread*
1 *cup crisp rice cereal*

Preheat the oven to 450 degrees. Combine the eggs, milk, cinnamon and salt in a shallow dish and mix well. Dip the bread slices into the egg mixture until thoroughly moistened. Drain the excess liquid. Sprinkle both sides of the bread lightly with the cereal. Place the bread slices on buttered baking sheets. Bake for 5 minutes on each side.

Note: Bread can soak, covered, in the egg mixture in the refrigerator for 8 to 10 hours.

Yield: 6 servings

Blueberry Cheese Strata

6 cups cubed bread

2 cups blueberries, fresh or frozen

⅓ cup sugar

1 cup shredded low-fat
   Swiss cheese

4 eggs, beaten, or an equivalent
   amount of egg substitute

2 cups low-fat milk

1 teaspoon vanilla extract

¼ teaspoon salt

½ teaspoon cinnamon

Vanilla yogurt or sour cream

Layer half the bread cubes, blueberries, sugar, cheese and remaining bread cubes in a buttered 8x8-inch baking dish. Combine the eggs, milk, vanilla and salt in a bowl and mix well. Pour the egg mixture over the bread. Sprinkle with cinnamon. Refrigerate, covered, for 6 to 24 hours. Preheat the oven to 325 degrees. Bake, uncovered, for 60 to 75 minutes or until a knife inserted in the center comes out clean. Let stand for 10 minutes before serving. Top with yogurt. Garnish with mint.

Yield: 10 servings

**Night Swan
Intracoastal B&B**

*Charles and Martha Nighswonger
512 South Riverside Drive
New Smyrna Beach, Florida 32168
(904) 423-4940 or
(800) 465-4261*

*Come watch the pelicans, dolphins,
sailboats, and yachts along the
Atlantic Intracoastal Waterway. We
are located between Daytona Beach
and Kennedy Space Center. Our
spacious three-story home has kept its
1906 character and charm. The
home is in the Historic District of
New Smyrna Beach and has
intricate, natural wood in every
room. Many of the fifteen rooms have
a private whirlpool tub and shower.
Enjoy a full breakfast in our dining
room or a continental breakfast on
the porch. Meeting space is available.*

Daytona Beach is often referred to as "the world's most famous beach." Its hard, sandy beaches have made auto racing famous since the 1930s. In 1914 John D. Rockefeller chose the area for the best year-round place to live. Also, the downtown Halifax Marina is the second largest on the East Coast. Daytona Beach is named after Mathias Day, who first bought property in 1870 where Daytona's two oldest homes make up Live Oak Inn.

One-Bowl Banana Bread

2 cups flour
½ cup sugar
2 teaspoons baking powder
1 teaspoon baking soda
½ teaspoon salt
2 eggs
2 or 3 very ripe bananas, mashed
⅓ cup vegetable oil
1 teaspoon vanilla extract

Preheat the oven to 350 degrees. Combine the flour, sugar, baking powder, baking soda, salt, eggs, bananas, oil and vanilla in a bowl and mix well. Pour into a greased 5x9-inch loaf pan or an 8- or 9-inch square baking pan. Bake for 40 minutes or until the bread tests done. Cool in the pan for 10 minutes. Remove to a wire rack to cool completely.

Yield: 9 to 12 servings

Apple Coffee Cake

2 cups baking mix
½ cup sugar
1 teaspoon baking powder
⅔ cup milk
1 egg
2 apples, finely chopped
⅓ cup packed brown sugar
⅓ cup flour
2 tablespoons butter
¼ cup chopped nuts

Preheat the oven to 375 degrees. Combine the baking mix, sugar, baking powder, milk, egg and apples in a bowl and mix well. Pour into a greased 8-inch square baking pan. Combine the brown sugar, flour, butter and chopped nuts in a small bowl and mix well. Sprinkle topping over the batter. Bake for 30 minutes.

Yield: 9 servings

Live Oak Inn
Jessie and Dell Glock
#444-448 South Beach Street
Daytona Beach, Florida 32114
(904) 252-4667

Relax and romance at one of Florida's top ten Historic Inns. Live Oak Inn offers the best of Daytona! The restful atmosphere of the Intracoastal Waterway and the excitement of the "World's Most Famous Beach" are only a mile away. Live Oak Inn features twelve guest rooms with their own private bath, TV, VCR, and telephone. Some rooms include balconies and in-room Jacuzzis.

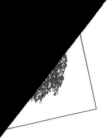
Lake Helen is located twenty-five miles southwest of Daytona Beach, thirty-five miles northeast of Orlando, and 100 years back in time. There are no traffic lights here, but there is a horse arena adjacent to the City Offices. This Historic District, which is on the National Register of Historic Places, offers a scene much as it was at the turn of the century. Lake Helen was founded in 1884 by Henry A. DeLand. He had long dreamed of developing a town around a pristine lake. When land became available in this area of high pine, he acquired about 1,000 acres, plotted streets, and named both the town and its principal lake for his daughter, Helen.

Chicken Puff

1 (6-ounce) package chicken-
   flavor stuffing mix
8 ounces Swiss cheese, shredded
1 cup chopped cooked chicken
3 tablespoons flour
2 tablespoons butter or margarine,
   melted
4 eggs, lightly beaten
3 cups milk

Preheat the oven to 350 degrees. Spread stuffing crumbs in a greased 9-inch square baking dish. Layer the cheese and chicken over the stuffing crumbs. Sprinkle with flour. Drizzle with the butter. Combine the eggs, milk and vegetable seasoning packet from the stuffing mix in a bowl and mix well. Pour over the layers. Bake, uncovered, for 1 hour or until nicely browned on top.

Note: Recipe may be assembled ahead and refrigerated.

Yield: 6 servings

Bread Pudding with Vanilla Custard Sauce

1 ½ (20-slice) loaves bread, torn
    into small pieces
4 cups milk, scalded
½ cup butter
1 ¼ cups sugar
4 eggs plus 2 egg whites,
    lightly beaten
½ teaspoon salt
2 teaspoons cinnamon
2 teaspoons vanilla extract
½ cup raisins (optional)
Vanilla Custard Sauce (below)

Preheat the oven to 350 degrees. Grease a
9x13-inch glass baking dish lightly. Place the
torn bread in a large bowl. Mix the scalded
milk and butter in a bowl until the butter
melts. Cool slightly. Add the milk mixture,
sugar, eggs, salt, cinnamon, vanilla and raisins
to the bread and mix well. Pour the mixture
into the prepared pan. Bake for 50 to
60 minutes or until browned. Pudding will
raise considerably but will fall as it cools.
Serve warm with Vanilla Custard Sauce.

Yield: 15 servings

Vanilla Custard Sauce

2 cups sugar
2 cups half-and-half
½ cup butter
2 egg yolks, beaten
2 teaspoons vanilla extract

Combine the sugar, half-and-half and butter in
a saucepan. Cook over medium heat until the
butter melts, stirring constantly. Cook for 3 to
4 minutes longer, stirring constantly. Stir a
small amount of the hot mixture into the
beaten eggs; stir the eggs into the hot mixture.
Cook the sauce for 2 to 3 minutes or until
thickened, stirring constantly. Remove from
heat. Stir in the vanilla.

Yield: 2 cups

Clauser's
Bed & Breakfast

Tom and Marge Clauser
201 East Kicklighter Road
Lake Helen, Florida 32744
(904) 228-0310 or
(800) 220-0310

Clauser's Bed & Breakfast is between
Orlando and Daytona Beach but in
secluded country charm, surrounded
by trees and gardens. The 1895
Main House and the 1994 Carriage
House have porches, private baths,
and Jacuzzis. Full breakfasts
are served. Country dinners are
served on the weekend. Be sure to
visit Sherlock's Pub.

Maitland

This quiet community is just five miles north of Orlando. Orange groves and the tourist trade thrived when the train line ended here in 1880. Incorporated in 1885, its natural beauty attracted many wealthy Northerners. Today, Maitland is well known for its cultural attractions—The Maitland Art Center, The Maitland Historical Museum, and The Waterhouse Residence Museum to name a few. Maitland also hosts two art festivals, one in the spring and one in the fall. They are held on the shores of beautiful Lake Lily, the "jewel" of the Maitland Cultural Corridor.

Mom's Lemon Bread

1/3 cup butter, softened
1 1/3 cups sugar
2 eggs
1/2 cup milk
1 1/2 cups flour
1 teaspoon baking powder
1/2 cup chopped nuts
Grated rind of 1 lemon
Juice of 1 lemon

Preheat the oven to 350 degrees. Cream the butter and 1 cup of the sugar in a bowl until light and fluffy. Add the eggs and milk and mix well. Add the flour and baking powder and mix well. Fold in the nuts and lemon rind. Pour into a greased 5x9-inch loaf pan. Bake for 60 minutes or until browned. Cool for 5 minutes in the pan. Combine the remaining 1/3 cup sugar and lemon juice in a small bowl and mix well. Pour over the bread. Let stand for 30 minutes. Remove from the pan and cool completely on a wire rack. Wrap in foil and let stand for several hours before serving.

Yield: 1 loaf

Stina's Omelet

4 eggs
¾ cup flour
2 cups milk
Shredded cheese (optional)
Cooked crumbled bacon (optional)
Diced cooked ham (optional)

Preheat the oven to 400 degrees. Whisk the eggs and flour in a bowl. Add the milk and mix well. Spray a 10-inch cast-iron skillet with nonstick cooking spray. Sprinkle the cheese, bacon and ham in the skillet. Pour the egg mixture over the top. Bake for 25 to 30 minutes or until puffed and browned.

Yield: 6 servings

Thurston House
Carole and Joe Ballard
851 Lake Avenue
Maitland, Florida 32751
(407) 539-1911 or
(800) 843-2721

Find a different escape at Thurston House—from lakefront porches, cozy rooms, and gardens to nearby antiquing, museums, and award-winning restaurants. Thurston House, North Orlando's finest bed-and-breakfast, has it all! It's perfect for business or pleasure; come see for yourself.

Sanford

Sanford, Florida, the historic waterfront gateway to Central Florida, is rich in heritage and folklore. Founded in 1877 by General Henry S. Sanford, the area was part of an original Spanish land grant. In the 1880s and 1890s riverboats plied the St. Johns River from Jacksonville to Sanford, connecting this city to the Atlantic Ocean. Commerce and new settlers to this interior frontier created quite a riverboat trade. At the turn of the century, Sanford became a thriving rail center, and James C. Higgins, superintendent of the railroad, lived in the house that is now The Higgins House Bed & Breakfast.

Higgins House Bread Pudding Supreme with Whiskey Sauce

1 (1-pound) loaf French or
    firm textured bread, cut into
    1-inch cubes
3 cups milk
½ cup butter, softened
1½ cups sugar
4 egg yolks
1 teaspoon vanilla extract
3 large baking apples, peeled,
    cored, thinly cut into
    round slices
1½ cups raisins
4 egg whites
Whiskey Sauce (page 69)

Preheat the oven to 350 degrees. Combine the bread cubes and milk in a large bowl. Let stand for 5 minutes. Cream the butter and 1 cup of the sugar in a large bowl until light and fluffy. Add the egg yolks and vanilla and mix well. Stir in the bread mixture. Layer ⅓ of the bread mixture, half the apples, half the raisins, ½ of the remaining bread mixture, remaining apples, remaining raisins and remaining bread mixture in a greased 8x8-inch baking dish. Place the baking dish in a larger baking pan. Pour the hottest tap water into the larger baking pan to a depth of 1 inch. Bake for 45 minutes or until the center is set. Beat the egg whites at high speed in a mixer bowl until soft peaks form. Beat in the remaining ½ cup sugar 1 tablespoon at a time at high speed until stiff peaks form. Remove the pudding from the pan of water. Spread the meringue over the hot pudding, sealing the meringue to the edges. Bake for 15 minutes or until golden brown. Serve warm with Whiskey Sauce.

Yield: 8 servings

Whiskey Sauce

1 egg, beaten
1 cup sugar
¼ cup butter
2 tablespoons bourbon
¾ cup whipping cream

Combine the egg, sugar and butter in a saucepan. Cook just until the mixture is thickened and begins to boil, stirring constantly. Remove from heat. Stir in the bourbon. Stir in the whipping cream gradually. Cool slightly before serving.

Yield: 1⅔ cups

Crab Meat and Mushroom Filling for Omelets

¼ cup butter
¼ cup flour
2 cups milk
2 teaspoons lemon juice
2 teaspoons prepared mustard
Salt and pepper to taste
Dash of Worcestershire sauce
⅓ cup white wine or sherry
4 egg yolks, beaten
1 pound fresh crab meat
1⅓ pounds fresh mushrooms

Melt the butter in a large skillet over medium heat. Whisk in the flour. Stir in the milk gradually. Cook until thickened, stirring constantly. Stir in the lemon juice, mustard, salt, pepper, Worcestershire sauce and wine. Stir a small amount of the hot mixture into the beaten egg yolks; stir the egg yolks into the hot mixture. Add the crabmeat and mushrooms and mix well. Use as a filling for a standard 3-egg omelet.

Yield: variable

The Higgins House Bed & Breakfast

Walt and Roberta Padgett
420 South Oak Avenue
Sanford, Florida 32771
(407) 324-9238 or
(800) 584-0014

Experience the charm and romance of a bygone era at this 1894 Victorian inn, located in historic Sanford near beautiful Lake Monroe and the St. Johns River. Three elegant guest rooms and "Cochranes Cottage" are available. Amenities include a Victorian garden, decks, and a hot tub. An expanded continental breakfast is served in our formal dining room. Antique shops are located nearby.

Orlando

Orlando is a vibrant, exciting destination that offers a dazzling array of vacation options, guaranteed to provide priceless memories that will last a lifetime. No matter how many times you visit Orlando, your next visit will be a completely different vacation each time. There is so much to do and see, one could never do it all in one vacation. If you want to pack as many exhilarating minutes as possible in your vacation menu, Orlando's attractions offer hair-raising rides, museums to open your eyes to cultural wonders, hundreds of golf courses to challenge your skills, and parks and gardens that invite you to experience Orlando's natural treasures.

Pasta Basul

Onions to taste
Cloves of garlic to taste
Olive oil
3 (16-ounce) cans tomato sauce
2 (16-ounce) cans early peas
6 cups water
Parsley flakes to taste
Oregano to taste
Fresh basil to taste
Salt and pepper to taste
1 pound small pasta

Mince the onions and garlic in a food processor. Sauté the onions and garlic in olive oil in a skillet until brown. Add the tomato sauce, peas, water, parsley flakes, oregano, basil, salt and pepper and mix well. Simmer for 20 minutes. Cook the pasta according to package directions; drain. Stir the pasta into the sauce. Serve immediately.

Yield: variable

Vegetarian Red Sauce

6 to 10 *cloves of garlic*

1 *extra-large onion*

¼ *cup olive oil*

2 *red bell peppers*

2 *green bell peppers*

1 *medium eggplant, peeled*

8 *ounces sliced fresh mushrooms*
   (optional)

2 *(28-ounce) cans tomato purée*

2 *(28-ounce) cans crushed*
   tomatoes

1 *(12-ounce) can tomato paste*

14 *cups water*

Salt and pepper to taste

Oregano to taste

Parsley leaves to taste

Garlic powder to taste

Fresh basil leaves to taste

2 *(10-ounce) packages Marjon*
   tofu crumbles

Chop the garlic cloves and onion in a food processor. Sauté the garlic and onion in olive oil in a very large saucepan until brown. Process the red peppers, green peppers, eggplant and mushrooms in a food processor until coarsely chopped; do not purée. Add the chopped vegetables, tomato purée, crushed tomatoes, tomato paste and water and mix well. Bring to a boil. Season with salt, pepper, oregano, parsley leaves, garlic powder and fresh basil. Simmer for 1 hour, stirring every 15 minutes. Add the tofu crumbles. Simmer for 1 hour or until dark red in color and vegetables are cooked through. Remove from heat. Let stand, covered, for 30 minutes. Serve over pasta and ravioli or use in lasagna and stuffed shells. Can be frozen.

Yield: variable

PerriHouse
Bed & Breakfast Inn

Nick and Angi Perretti
10417 Centurion Court
Orlando, Florida 32836
(407) 876-4830 or
(800) 780-4830

PerriHouse is a private, rustic country estate inn, located on four secluded acres. Walt Disney World is just five minutes away, and the Convention Center is only 10 minutes away. Birdwatching is encouraged on the quiet, tranquil grounds of the inn, which is themed as a bird sanctuary. Eight guest rooms feature private baths, private entrances, televisions, and telephones. Families are welcome. The inn also features a pool and spa. An upscale continental breakfast buffet is served.

Winter Garden

There are not many "one-street towns" left in Florida . . . but Tildenville is one of them. Luther F. Tilden, one of Central Florida's original citrus growers and builder of the home now known as Meadow Marsh, was the founder of this quaint little area called Tildenville back in 1877. The neighboring town of Oakland was once larger than Orlando, but now also remains as a one-street town. A wonderful "get away" from the hustle-bustle of today awaits you fourteen miles west of downtown Orlando in these dots on the map where huge oak trees canopy the streets and the folks still have time to be neighborly.

Cream of Carrot Soup

3 cups shredded carrots
¼ cup chopped onion
¼ cup chopped celery
4 cups chicken broth
4 cups whipping cream or
half-and-half
Salt and white pepper to taste

Combine the carrots, onion, celery and chicken broth in a saucepan. Simmer until the vegetables are tender-crisp. Remove from heat. Set aside. Pour the whipping cream in a saucepan. Cook until the whipping cream thickens to the desired consistency; do not boil. Stir in the vegetable mixture. Season with salt and white pepper.

Yield: 4 servings

Holiday Nut Bread

2¹/₂ cups flour

1 teaspoon baking soda

1 tablespoon baking powder

1¹/₂ teaspoons salt

1 cup sugar

¹/₃ cup vegetable oil

2 eggs

³/₄ cup sour milk

1 cup mashed bananas

¹/₂ cup finely chopped peeled
    apples

1 cup maraschino cherries

1 cup chopped nuts

Preheat the oven to 350 degrees. Mix the flour, baking soda, baking powder and salt together. Combine the sugar, vegetable oil and eggs in a bowl and mix well. Add the dry ingredients alternately with the milk and bananas, mixing well after each addition. Stir in the apples, cherries and nuts. Pour into a greased loaf pan. Bake for 70 minutes or until a wooden pick inserted in the center comes out clean, covering the top of the bread with foil if needed to prevent burning. Cool in the pan for 10 minutes. Remove to a wire rack to cool completely.

Yield: 1 loaf

Meadow Marsh
Bed & Breakfast

Cavelle and John Pawlack
940 Tildenville School Road
Winter Garden, Florida 34787
(407) 656-2064 or
(888) 656-2064

Meadow Marsh, a beautiful historic home, is situated on twelve acres just west of downtown Orlando. Two of the suites and the cottage have two-person whirlpools. Two of the rooms have old-fashioned tubs/showers. A three-course breakfast is served each morning in the tearoom, which overlooks a vast meadow. The house is surrounded by 100-year-old oaks. Porch swings, nature walks, games, or the adjacent "Tails-to-Trails" path make this a place to relax, leaving your stress behind. Meadow Marsh is close to all Central Florida attractions, but far from the rush in its quiet one-street neighborhood. Do come . . . Discover old Florida while exploring the new!

Mount Dora

The first people to inhabit Mount Dora were the Indians of the Timuca tribe, as long as 500 years ago. The first Europeans to see the area were possibly the Spanish, who marched through Florida in the sixteenth century and made notice of the Timuca tribe. There are records of homesteaders and squatters in this area throughout the eighteenth and nineteenth centuries. Mount Dora was officially founded in the 1800s, along the banks of Lake Dora.

Brunch Banana Cake

5 *tablespoons butter*
1 *(2-layer) package coconut pecan or almond frosting mix*
1 *cup rolled oats*
1 *cup sour cream*
4 *eggs*
2 *large bananas*
1 *(2-layer) package yellow cake mix*

Preheat the oven to 350 degrees. Grease and lightly flour a 10-inch tube pan or a bundt pan. Melt the butter in a saucepan. Stir in the frosting mix and oats until crumbly. Set aside. Combine the sour cream, eggs and bananas in a mixer bowl. Beat at medium speed until smooth. Add the cake mix. Beat at medium speed for 2 minutes. Layer the batter and frosting mixture ⅓ at a time in the prepared pan. Bake for 50 minutes or until the cake tests done. Cool in the pan for 10 minutes. Invert onto a serving plate.

Yield: 10 servings

Spaghetti Salad

8 ounces spaghetti
1 cucumber, thinly sliced
1 green bell pepper, chopped
1 (1-pound) package cherry
    tomatoes, halved
1½ ounces Salad Supreme
    seasoning
1 (8-ounce) bottle Italian
    salad dressing

Prepare spaghetti using package directions and drain. Let stand until cool. Combine the spaghetti, cucumber, green pepper and cherry tomatoes in a bowl and mix well. Sprinkle with the Salad Supreme seasoning. Pour the Italian salad dressing over the vegetables. Toss to coat. Refrigerate, covered, for 8 to 10 hours. Stir before serving.

Yield: 8 servings

**Farnsworth House
Bed & Breakfast**

Dick and Sandy Shelton
1029 East 5th Avenue
Mount Dora, Florida 32757
(352) 735-1894

Farnsworth House is located on
one and one-half acres in the historic
town of Mount Dora with its
many boutiques and antique shops.
It was built in 1886 with three suites
and two efficiencies, each decorated
in a unique theme with private baths
and kitchens. Guests can enjoy
the large screened porch,
living/dining room, and a hot tub
in a screened gazebo.

Crazy Lemon Muffins

2 cups flour
½ cup sugar
1 teaspoon baking powder
½ teaspoon baking soda
¼ teaspoon salt
3 tablespoons melted margarine
1 teaspoon grated lemon rind
¼ cup fresh lemon juice
2 large eggs
1 (8-ounce) carton lemon
   low-fat yogurt
1 cup craisins, or desired amount
   of poppy seeds
1 teaspoon vanilla extract
2 tablespoons fresh lemon juice
   (optional)
Confectioners' sugar (optional)

Preheat the oven to 400 degrees. Mix the flour, sugar, baking powder, baking soda and salt in a medium bowl. Make a well in the center. Whisk the margarine, lemon rind, ¼ cup lemon juice, eggs, yogurt, craisins and vanilla in a small bowl. Add to the dry ingredients, stirring just until moistened. Spoon the batter into greased muffin cups, filling ⅔ full. Bake for 15 to 20 minutes or until the muffins test done. Cool in the pan for 10 minutes. Remove to a wire rack to cool completely. Mix 2 tablespoons lemon juice with enough confectioners' sugar to make of the desired consistency in a small bowl. Spread the glaze on the muffins.

Yield: 12 muffins

Magnolia Inn French Toast

1 or 2 medium French baguettes
   or loaves
4 large eggs
½ cup premium vanilla ice cream,
   melted
¼ cup fresh orange juice
1 tablespoon vanilla extract
1 tablespoon cinnamon
Pinch of nutmeg
Butter

Cut the bread into ¾-inch slices, discarding the ends. Arrange the bread in a single layer in a large dish. Combine the eggs, ice cream, orange juice, vanilla, cinnamon and nutmeg in a medium bowl and mix well. Pour over the bread slices. Let stand for a few minutes. Heat the griddle. Melt a small amount of butter on the griddle. Add the soaked bread. Cook until brown on both sides, turning once. Serve with fresh berries on top, heated blueberry and maple syrups and a sprinkling of lemon zest, or serve with apple slices cooked in butter, brown sugar and cinnamon.

Yield: 8 servings

Magnolia Inn
Gerry and Lita Johnson
347 East Third Avenue
Mount Dora, Florida 32757
(352) 735-3800 or
(800) 776-2112

Southern hospitality and charm at its finest are found at Magnolia Inn. Lounge in a hammock, swing under the magnolia, or unwind in the gazebo spa. Explore small-town pleasures of quaint antique shops, boutiques, and exceptional dining. Carriage rides, trolley tours, golf, tennis, and water sports are also available. Enjoy elegant rooms with private baths and hearty homemade breakfasts. Magnolia Inn is thirty miles from Orlando and the beaches. It's perfect for romantic getaways.

Mount Dora

Mount Dora is a quaint
little town reminiscent of a seaside
New England village. In the late
1800s, Mount Dora was the
southernmost point in Florida's
interior that you could reach by
steamboat from the Atlantic. It
has become a mecca for
craftspeople, antiquers, and
artists of all types. It is known all
over Florida for its fine shopping,
dining, and lodging. Many have
said, "It is like stepping back
100 years in time."

Nancy's Baked Fruit Clafouti

2 tablespoons butter
1 cup sliced fruit of choice
1 1/4 cups pancake mix
1/2 cup whole milk
1 egg
Maple syrup

Preheat the oven to 350 degrees. Melt the
butter in a glass pie plate. Swirl the pie plate
to allow the butter to coat the bottom and
side. Place the fruit in the pie plate. Combine
the pancake mix, milk and egg in a small bowl
and mix well. Pour the batter over the fruit.
Bake for 25 minutes or until the top starts to
brown. Remove from the oven. Loosen the
clafouti with a grapefruit knife. Invert onto a
large serving platter. Serve with maple syrup.

Note: Marinate sour fruit in lots of sugar for
8 to 10 hours in the refrigerator and pour off
the excess liquid before using.

Yield: 8 servings

Lindsay's Fresh Mango Bread

1 ½ cups flour
¼ teaspoon salt
¾ teaspoon baking soda
¾ teaspoon baking powder
1 ¼ cups sugar
2 eggs
6 tablespoons butter
¼ cup milk
⅓ cup mashed mango
6 tablespoons chopped nuts
1 tablespoon orange juice
1 tablespoon honey

Preheat the oven to 350 degrees. Sift the flour, salt, baking soda, baking powder and sugar together in a large bowl. Add the eggs, butter and milk and mix well. Do not overmix as it makes the dough tough. Fold in the mango and nuts. Pour batter into a greased loaf pan. Bake for 50 to 60 minutes or until the bread tests done. Combine the orange juice and honey in a small bowl and mix well. Brush on top of the bread. Cool in the pan on a wire rack for 15 minutes.

Yield: 1 loaf

Mount Dora Historic Inn

Lindsay and Nancy Richards
221 East Fourth Avenue
Mount Dora, Florida 32757
(800) 927-6344 *or*
(352) 735-1212

Relive the elegance of the past in a turn-of-the-century Mount Dora bed-and-breakfast, nestled in a secluded romantic setting. Amenities include beautifully appointed rooms, separate baths, full gourmet breakfast, turndown service, and period antiques. Enjoy complete comfort and tranquility. Walk to antique shops, specialty shops, a nature boardwalk, carriage rides, and gourmet restaurants.

Lake Wales

In the mornings, as the sun touches the sky near mist-shrouded shorelines and birds in ancient oaks begin their wake-up songs, both Lake Wales locals and visitors alike are inspired to venture outside and explore their world. Enjoy an early morning walk through our beautiful gardens, visit a world-renowned bell tower, enjoy an outstanding play, or meander through a lovingly preserved downtown district. During the season, you might relive the life of Christ at the famed Black Hills Passion Play, enjoy the annual Art Show by the lake, experience music by artists from around the world during the International Carillon Festival, or party at the February Mardi Gras celebration.

Chalet Suzanne's Broiled Grapefruit

1 *grapefruit, at room temperature*
3 *tablespoons butter or margarine*
1 *teaspoon sugar*
4 *tablespoons cinnamon-sugar*
2 *cooked chicken livers (optional)*

Slice the grapefruit into halves. Cut the membrane around the center. Cut around each section half close to the membrane so that the fruit is completely loosened from the shell. Fill the center of each half with 1½ tablespoons of butter. Sprinkle ½ teaspoon sugar and 2 tablespoons cinnamon-sugar over each half. Place the grapefruit in a shallow baking pan. Broil just until the tops are brown and the grapefruit is bubbling. Remove from the oven. Top each half with a chicken liver.

Yield: 2 servings

Chalet Suzanne's Gâteau Christina

6 egg whites
2 cups sugar
⅓ cup ground blanched almonds
2 tablespoons sweetened cocoa
1 cup butter, softened
4 ounces semisweet chocolate,
    melted

Preheat the oven to 250 degrees. Cut foil into four 8-inch circles and grease each lightly. Place the foil circles on a large baking sheet. Beat 4 of the egg whites in a mixer bowl until soft peaks form. Add 1½ cups of the sugar and the almonds gradually, beating constantly until stiff peaks form. Spread each foil circle evenly with the meringue. Bake for 15 minutes or until the meringues are dry. Turn meringues over carefully. Bake for 5 minutes longer. Beat the remaining 2 egg whites in a double boiler over hot water until foamy. Add the remaining ½ cup sugar, cocoa, butter and chocolate gradually, beating constantly until thick and creamy. Remove from heat and cool. Remove the foil from the meringue circles. Alternate the meringue circles with the chocolate filling until all ingredients are used, ending with the chocolate filling. Press lightly to make the layers fit together. Refrigerate, covered, for 24 hours or longer.

Yield: 1 gâteau

Chalet Suzanne

Vita Hinshaw
U.S. 27 North and
Chalet Suzanne Road
Lake Wales, Florida 33853-7060
(941) 676-6011 or
(800) 433-6011

Chalet Suzanne is a delightful thirty-room country inn, located in a National Historic District. Featuring romantic lodging and legendary fare, the inn is surrounded by fragrant orange groves. Among its many awards and recognitions are Travel Holiday & Golden Spoon Dining Awards, the Uncle Ben's Top Ten Country Inns award (of which the inn is a national winner), the Mobil Guide 4-star listing, and being chosen "Most Romantic." Family owned and operated since 1931, the AAA-rated inn provides a quiet relaxing atmosphere with a lounge, pool, and airstrip. Gifts, ceramics, and antiques are available for purchase.

The Gulf Coast

One long perfect beach along Florida's quiet coast...Gulf Coast enthusiasts would go nowhere else. Bridges connect one island to the next, beginning in Clearwater and ending in Naples. Along the beaches of the Gulf Coast are fewer hotels and high rises, more private homes and open spaces. Some of the best shelling in the country can be found along the beaches of Venice. For daytime excursions, the region is full of museums, aquariums, and attractions; yet each day ends in an orange-pink sunset.

Just thirty minutes farther south and you're in another world—the Florida Everglades. Nature enthusiasts can enjoy the wealth of ecological diversity in the region and silence undisturbed but for the roar of an airboat engine.

Florida
Gulf Coast

Anna Maria Island

Originally settled in 1892, Anna Maria Island is surrounded by the Gulf of Mexico, Tampa Bay, and Sarasota Bay. Development of this lush tropical island started to bloom in the early 1900s, as John Roser and his son, Charles, built the first church, Roser Memorial, in 1913. Charles Roser, a baker from Ohio when not wintering on the island, was the creator of the well-known cookie, the "Fig Newton."

"HH" Buttermilk Pancakes

2 *cups flour*
2 *teaspoons sugar*
2 *teaspoons (heaping) baking powder*
1 *teaspoon baking soda*
1 *teaspoon salt*
2 *eggs*
2 *cups buttermilk*
¼ *cup vegetable oil*
Brown Sugar Syrup (below)

Combine the flour, sugar, baking powder, baking soda and salt in a bowl and mix well. Combine the eggs, buttermilk and oil in a small bowl and mix well. Add to the dry ingredients. Stir until moist but slightly lumpy; do not overmix. Pour ¼ cup at a time onto a hot lightly greased griddle. Bake until brown on both sides. Serve with Brown Sugar Syrup.

Yield: 8 servings

Brown Sugar Syrup

¼ *cup butter*
⅔ *cup packed brown sugar*
⅓ *cup light corn syrup*
¼ *cup water*

Melt the butter in a saucepan. Stir in the brown sugar, corn syrup and water. Cook over medium heat until the syrup thickens, stirring constantly.

Yield: ¾ cup

Bacon Crab Meat Rolls

¼ cup chopped tomatoes
1 egg, well beaten
1 cup flaked crab meat, drained
½ cup fine bread crumbs
1 teaspoon parsley
1 teaspoon lemon juice
¼ teaspoon salt
¼ teaspoon Worcestershire sauce
Dash of hot pepper sauce
Bacon slices, cut into halves

Combine the tomatoes and egg in a bowl and mix well. Add the crab meat, bread crumbs, parsley, lemon juice, salt, Worcestershire sauce and hot pepper sauce and mix well. Roll the mixture into 2-inch logs. Wrap each log with half a slice of bacon. Place on a rack in a broiler pan. Broil 5 inches from the heat source for 10 minutes or until cooked through.

Yield: 4 servings

Harrington House Beachfront B&B

Frank and Jo Davis
5626 Gulf Drive
Holmes Beach, Florida 34217
(941) 778-5444

The charm of old Florida architecture and the casual elegance of beachfront living are beautifully combined at our one-of-a-kind bed-and-breakfast guest house on Anna Maria Island. Built in 1925, this lovingly restored home has twelve charming bedrooms, each with its own unique decor and private bath. Leave the crowds behind, and enjoy the congenial hospitality of Harrington House.

Englewood

Englewood, Florida was named in 1884 by Herbert Nicholas and his two brothers who moved there from Englewood, Illinois. The Nicholas brothers had high hopes of building a business growing lemons, which were in high demand as a cure for scurvy at the time. The "worst-ever" freezes of 1894 and 1895 quickly ended their plans.

Plantain and Wheat Germ-Crusted Pompano with Paw-Paw Escabeche and Mango-Pepper Butter

½ cup vegetable oil
1 plantain, sliced very thinly lengthwise
1 cup honey wheat germ
Grated rind of 1 lime
Pinch of allspice
Pinch of cayenne
Pinch of salt
2 (7-ounce) fillets of pompano or snapper
Juice of 1 lime
1 cup buttermilk
1 tablespoon honey
Paw-Paw Escabeche (page 87)
Mango-Pepper Butter (page 87)

Heat the oil in a saucepan to 350 degrees. Add the plantain slices; do not overcrowd. Fry until crisp. Remove to paper towels to drain. Reserve 2 tablespoons of the pan drippings. Place plantain slices in a food processor container. Pulse until of medium grain. Add the wheat germ, lime rind, allspice, cayenne and salt. Pulse to mix. Pat the fish fillets dry. Combine the lime juice, buttermilk and honey in a small bowl and mix well. Dip the fish in the buttermilk mixture. Coat with the plantain mixture, pressing the crumbs onto the fish. Heat the reserved pan drippings in a skillet. Add the fillets. Sauté until golden on each side. Place a large spoonful of the warm Paw-Paw Escabeche on each ovenproof individual serving plate. Add a fish fillet. Place a slice of the Mango-Pepper Butter on top of each fish. Preheat the broiler. Broil for 15 seconds. Serve immediately.

Yield: 2 servings

Paw-Paw Escabeche

1 unripe green papaya
½ Florida sweet onion
1 red bell pepper
1 poblano or green bell pepper
½ plantain, peeled
2 tablespoons vegetable oil
½ tablespoon minced garlic
½ jalapeño, seeded, minced
1 cup fresh orange juice
1 tablespoon lime juice
½ tablespoon tamarind syrup
¼ cup rice wine vinegar
Salt and white pepper to taste

Cut the papaya, onion, red pepper, poblano pepper and plantain into slices 3 inches long by ¼ inch thick. Sauté the plantain and onion in the oil in a skillet over medium-high heat for 4 minutes. Add the red pepper, poblano pepper and papaya. Sauté for 2 minutes. Add the garlic and jalapeño. Sauté for 1 minute. Add the orange juice. Cook until the juice is reduced by half. Add the lime juice, tamarind syrup and rice wine vinegar and mix well. Cook until the juice is reduced by half. Remove from the heat and keep warm. Add salt and white pepper to taste.

Yield: 2 cups

Mango-Pepper Butter

¼ cup chopped fresh mango
½ tablespoon minced shallot
1 red jalapeño, seeded, chopped
1 teaspoon minced gingerroot
1 cup unsalted butter, cubed,
    softened
1 teaspoon minced garlic
Grated rind of 1 lime
Grated rind of 1 orange
Pinch of allspice
Pinch of salt
Juice of 1 lime
Juice of 1 orange
½ tablespoon thinly sliced
    scallions
1 tablespoon minced cilantro

Sauté the mango, shallot, jalapeño and gingerroot in 1 tablespoon of the butter for 30 seconds. Add the garlic, lime rind, orange rind, allspice and salt. Sauté for 30 seconds. Add the lime juice and orange juice. Sauté for 1 minute or until almost all of the liquid has evaporated. Remove from the heat and cool. Add the scallions and cilantro to the mango mixture. Place the remaining butter in a bowl. Fold in the mango mixture. Place the mixture on a sheet of waxed or parchment paper. Roll tightly into a cylinder and twist the ends. Refrigerate until ready to use.

Yield: ¼ cup

Manasota Beach Club

James and Desa Buffum
7660 Manasota Key Road
Englewood, Florida 34223
(941) 474-2614

The Manasota Beach Club is a seasonal full American-plan resort, located directly on the Gulf of Mexico. Outstanding quality food is prepared fresh daily by a friendly professional staff. Cottages and rooms are situated in a 26-acre natural tropical landscape. A residential beach, nature trails, tennis courts, six-wicket croquet, and a swimming pool, amid palm trees, palmettos, and moss-covered live oaks, create an ideal vacation setting.

Naples

Relax under coconut palms near white sand beaches. Naples is a tropical getaway, renowned for its fabulous shopping, gourmet restaurants, and art galleries, but it is just minutes from the edge of the Florida Everglades. As a matter of fact, the "swamp buggy" was first designed and built here by Ed Frank in the 1940s. In 1932 Charles Lindbergh landed his airplane on the Fifth Avenue Golf Course in order to buy supplies at the local commissary.

Strawberries with Crème Fraîche

½ *cup whipping cream*
½ *cup sour cream*
4 *cups fresh strawberry halves*
¼ *cup packed brown sugar*

Combine the whipping cream and sour cream in a small bowl and mix well. Let stand, covered, at room temperature for 5 to 12 hours or until the mixture thickens. Refrigerate for 24 hours. Place the strawberries in 8 individual serving bowls. Top with the crème fraîche. Sprinkle with brown sugar.

Yield: 8 servings

Fresh Apple Cake

2 eggs, beaten
2 cups sugar
½ cup vegetable oil
1 teaspoon vanilla extract
2 cups flour
2 teaspoons baking soda
2 teaspoons cinnamon
1 teaspoon salt
4 Jonathan apples, peeled, diced
Cream Cheese Icing (below)

Preheat the oven to 350 degrees. Combine the eggs, sugar, oil and vanilla in a bowl and mix well. Sift the flour, baking soda, cinnamon and salt together. Stir the dry ingredients into the egg mixture and mix well. Stir in the apples; batter will be stiff. Pour into a lightly greased 9x13-inch cake pan. Bake for 40 to 50 minutes or until the cake tests done. Cool. Frost with Cream Cheese Icing.

Yield: 12 servings

Cream Cheese Icing

8 ounces cream cheese, softened
1½ cups confectioners' sugar
1 tablespoon butter
1 teaspoon vanilla extract
1 teaspoon salt

Combine the cream cheese, confectioners' sugar, butter, vanilla and salt in a bowl and mix until smooth.

Yield: 2 cups

The Inn by the Sea

Will and Tara Jones
287 Eleventh Avenue South
Naples, Florida 34102-7022
(941) 649-4124 or
(800) 584-1268

Surrounded by coconut palms, The Inn by the Sea is a charming tropical home with five guest rooms, all with private baths. Just two blocks from the Gulf, the Inn affords its guests walking access to miles of white sand beaches, plus fabulous shopping, restaurants, and galleries in Old Naples. It is also listed on the National Register of Historic Places. Bicycles and beach chairs are provided.

Old Florida is still present in Everglades City. Indian trading posts, museums, and wonderful wildlife are part of this quiet fishing village in the heart of the Everglades. The enchanted grassland is world renowned, but don't be startled to hear the roaring sounds of an airboat or swamp buggy cruising by!

Chicken Everglades

2 *tablespoons oregano*
2 *tablespoons basil*
1 *tablespoon Everglades seasoning mix*
3 *tablespoons grated Parmesan cheese*
Salt and pepper to taste
4 *boneless skinless chicken breasts*
Olive oil for browning
Oregano to taste
8 *fresh whole basil leaves*
1 *teaspoon paprika*
Fresh parsley to taste
1 *(28-ounce) can tomatoes, chopped*
1/2 *cup grated Parmesan cheese*

Preheat the oven to 350 degrees. Combine 2 tablespoons oregano, 2 tablespoons basil, Everglades seasoning mix, 3 tablespoons Parmesan cheese, salt and pepper in a shallow dish and mix well. Dredge the chicken in the seasoning mixture until coated. Heat the oil in a skillet. Add the chicken. Cook until the chicken is brown, turning once; do not burn. Place the chicken in a glass baking dish. Sprinkle with pepper and oregano to taste. Place 2 basil leaves on each chicken breast. Sprinkle with paprika. Cover the chicken breasts with parsley. Sprinkle with tomatoes and 1/2 cup Parmesan cheese. Bake, uncovered, for 1 hour or until the chicken is cooked through.

Yield: 4 servings

Topping for Fresh Fruit

1 cup vanilla yogurt
½ cup applesauce
Nutmeg to taste
Cinnamon to taste

Combine the yogurt, applesauce, nutmeg and cinnamon in a bowl and mix well. Refrigerate, covered, until chilled. Serve over fresh fruit.

Yield: 1 ½ cups

On the Banks of the Everglades

Patty Flick Richards
201 West Broadway
Everglades City, Florida 34139
(888) 431-1977 or
(941) 695-3151

Tranquility nestled in the "Bank of Everglades Building," which was chartered in 1923, this old Florida-style bed-and-breakfast enjoys the serenity of the Everglades. The building was the original and only bank in Collier County, Florida until 1962. Birds, reptiles, and roaring sounds of airboats can all be found here. Breakfast is a safe bet, served in the walk-in vault! The Checking Department, Foreclosures Department, and Vice President's Suite are a few of our twelve rooms.

Tropical Southeast Florida

Long the vacationland of the Northern
elite, the southeast coast is a blend of
high-profile, fashionable cities, beautiful
beaches, and golf resorts. Diverse culture,
nightlife, and shopping blend with quiet towns,
outstanding restaurants, and outdoor sports,
including the "Sport Fish Capital" of the
world. Travel inland just minutes and see an
"Old Florida" time has forgotten. Citrus and
sugarcane farms, with an intricate network of
canals, thrive alongside ranches, swamps, and
wildlife. Small towns dot the banks of
Okeechobee, the nation's largest lake.

Southeast
Florida

Indiantown

Indiantown was settled by Francis Marion Platt in the late 1890s, after he was acquitted of the cold-blooded murder of another rancher. Indiantown was originally named Annie for Platt's wife in 1902, when he became postmaster of the small town. In 1924 S. Davies Warfield brought his Seaboard Airline Railroad through the small town and decided to settle. He built the Seminole Inn in 1926. Ten years after his death, the land was bought by Indian Town Development Corporation and Annie became Indiantown.

Coconut-Pecan Sweet Potato Casserole

4 cups milk

6 fresh cooked sweet potatoes, peeled

½ cup unsalted butter

2 eggs

3½ cups packed light brown sugar

¼ cup sugar

1 teaspoon cinnamon

2 teaspoons vanilla extract

4 cups coconut

1 cup pecan pieces

Preheat the oven to 350 degrees. Combine the milk, sweet potatoes, butter, eggs, 1½ cups of the brown sugar, sugar, cinnamon and vanilla in a bowl and mix until light and fluffy. Pour into a buttered 9x13-inch baking pan. Sprinkle with coconut, pecan pieces and the remaining 2 cups brown sugar. Bake for 45 minutes.

Yield: 15 servings

Southern Pecan-Encrusted Chicken with Warm Berry Sauce

1 *cup flour*
1/2 *cup pecan pieces*
Boneless skinless chicken breasts
Butter
Warm Berry Sauce (below)

Preheat the oven to 350 degrees. Combine the flour and pecan pieces in a food processor container. Pulse until pecan pieces are minced and mixed with flour. Coat the chicken breasts with the flour mixture. Melt enough butter in a skillet to cover the bottom. Add the chicken breasts. Cook until brown, turning once. Spray a baking pan with nonstick cooking spray. Place the chicken breasts in the baking pan. Bake for 20 minutes or until cooked through. Drizzle some of the Warm Berry Sauce over individual serving plates. Place the chicken breasts on the prepared plates. Drizzle with the remaining Warm Berry Sauce.

Yield: variable

Warm Berry Sauce

1 *cup frozen berries of choice*
2 *cups sugar*

Combine the berries and sugar in a saucepan. Cook over medium heat until of the desired consistency, stirring occasionally.

Yield: 1 1/2 cups

Seminole Country Inn

Jonnie Wall-Williams
15885 Southwest
Warfield Boulevard
Indiantown, Florida 34956
(561) 597-3777

Only thirty miles from Palm Beach but light years away, the Seminole Country Inn instantly takes you back to a slower, more gracious time in rural Florida, a time of "Old Southern Hospitality." Pecky Cypress ceilings, spiral staircases, pine hardwood floors, and antiques remind you of Grandma's house. Come to our inn. Come home. We are waiting for you.

Fort Pierce

Fort Pierce, on beautiful North Hutchinson Island, was named after Lieutenant Colonel Benjamin Kendrick Pierce, U.S. Army. His brother was Franklin Pierce, fourteenth President of the United States. Today this still unspoiled, uncrowded barrier island boasts nature trails, lots of fishing, canoeing through the Indian River Lagoon, and horseback riding on the beach.

Chocolate Bread Pudding

*6 cups lightly packed ½-inch
    cubes trimmed egg bread*
2½ cups half-and-half
*8 ounces semisweet chocolate,
    chopped*
4 large egg yolks
¼ cup sugar
1 teaspoon vanilla extract
1 teaspoon salt
Lightly sweetened whipped cream

Divide the bread cubes evenly among eight ¾-cup custard cups. Pour the half-and-half into a heavy medium saucepan. Bring to a simmer over medium heat. Remove from heat. Add the chocolate. Stir until melted and smooth. Add the egg yolks, sugar, vanilla and salt. Whisk until blended. Pour over the bread cubes, dividing evenly. Press down on bread cubes with back of spoon to saturate bread completely. Let stand at room temperature for 25 minutes. Preheat the oven to 325 degrees. Cover custard cups loosely with aluminum foil. Bake for 30 minutes or until set and a knife inserted into centers comes out with some moist pudding still attached. Serve warm with a dollop of whipped cream.

Note: Serve as a Valentine's Day dessert by baking in a heart-shaped pan and covering with whipped cream!

Yield: 8 servings

Blintz Soufflé

1 pound cottage cheese
3 ounces cream cheese, softened
1/4 cup melted butter or margarine
1/3 cup sugar
1/2 cup flour
3 eggs
1/2 teaspoon fresh lemon juice
1/2 teaspoon baking powder
1/2 teaspoon cinnamon
Blueberry Sauce (below)

Preheat the oven to 350 degrees. Combine the cottage cheese, cream cheese, butter and sugar in a medium bowl and mix well. Add the flour, eggs, lemon juice and baking powder and mix thoroughly. Spoon into a greased 8x8-inch baking pan. Sprinkle with cinnamon. Bake for 45 minutes or until light brown around the edges and springy to the touch. Serve with Blueberry Sauce.

Note: For Strawberry Sauce, mix sliced strawberries with a small amount of orange marmalade.

Yield: 4 servings

Blueberry Sauce

1 cup frozen blueberries,
   raspberries, cherries or peaches
1/4 cup orange juice
1 tablespoon honey
1 tablespoon cornstarch
1 tablespoon cold water

Combine the blueberries, orange juice and honey in a saucepan. Dissolve the cornstarch in the cold water in a bowl. Add to the blueberry mixture. Cook until thickened, stirring constantly.

Yield: 1 cup

The Mellon Patch Inn
Arthur and Andrea Mellon
3601 North A1A
North Hutchinson Island,
Florida 34949
800 MLN PTCH

Escape to a beach setting. Let us pamper you. Wake up to freshly ground coffee and a full gourmet breakfast. The ocean is just across the street. Explore the parks and nature preserve. Play tennis, golf, boat, and fish from our dock. Poke through the little-known galleries of affordable art, and shop for antiques. Enjoy a cool drink as the sun sets over the Indian River.

Stuart

The Indian River lured Hubert W. Bessey and his brother from Ohio to be part of the first settlers in the late 1800s. Aboriginal Indians roamed this area for at least 10,000 years prior to that time. Mr. Bessey was an early pineapple planter, as well as a house builder and boat builder. The Stuart area was originally settled as pineapple plantations. By the mid-twentieth century almost all the plantations disappeared due to severe weather conditions, the railroad, and Cuban competition.

HarborFront Ambrosia

2 Navel oranges
1 large red grapefruit
1 ripe carambola (star fruit)
1/4 cup grated coconut
4 to 6 maraschino cherries

Peel and section the oranges and grapefruit. Cut the carambola into 1/4-inch slices. Combine the orange and grapefruit sections, carambola slices and grated coconut in a bowl and mix well. Spoon into fluted sherbet dishes. Top each with a maraschino cherry.

Yield: 4 to 6 servings

Mango Custard Tarts

1 sheet of frozen puff pastry
   or pie pastry
3 eggs
1 cup sugar
1 teaspoon grated lemon rind or
   lime rind
1 cup fresh mango purée
¼ cup heavy cream
Lightly sweetened whipped cream

Preheat the oven to 375 degrees. Spray 6 muffin cups with nonstick cooking spray. Cut the puff pastry to fit the muffin cups. Line the muffin cups with the pastry. Whisk the eggs, sugar and lemon rind together in a bowl. Stir in the mango purée and cream and mix well. Pour into the prepared muffin cups. Bake for 12 to 15 minutes or until puffed and golden brown and a knife inserted in the centers comes out clean.

Note: May substitute a pie pan or tart pan with a removable bottom for the muffin cups. Bake for 25 to 30 minutes.

Yield: 6 servings

Stuart

Sailfishing is so intense offshore that it has earned Stuart the title of "Sailfish Capital of the World." Fishing is so superb that it has attracted presidents, such as Chester A. Arthur, William Howard Taft, Theodore Roosevelt, Grover Cleveland, and Warren G. Harding. There are hundreds of edible species swimming in the depths of the rivers.

Easy Brunch Casserole

1 (12-ounce) package bulk
  sausage
1 (6-ounce) package onion-garlic
  croutons
6 eggs, beaten, or an equivalent
  amount of egg substitute
1 cup milk
2 to 3 cups shredded sharp
  Cheddar cheese
1 (10-ounce) can cream of
  mushroom soup
1 (3-ounce) can mushrooms,
  drained

Brown the sausage in a skillet, stirring until crumbly; drain. Sprinkle croutons in a 9x13-inch baking pan sprayed with nonstick cooking spray. Sprinkle the sausage over the croutons. Combine the eggs with ½ cup of the milk in a bowl and mix well. Pour over the sausage. Sprinkle with cheese. Mix the soup, remaining ½ cup milk and mushrooms in a bowl. Pour over the cheese. Refrigerate, covered with plastic wrap, for 8 to 10 hours. Preheat the oven to 325 degrees. Bake for 1 hour.

Yield: 6 to 8 servings

Brunch Oven Omelet

¼ *cup margarine or butter*
18 *eggs*
1 *cup sour cream or fat-free*
    sour cream
1 *cup milk*
2 *teaspoons salt or seasoned salt*
¼ *cup chopped green onions*

Preheat the oven to 325 degrees. Melt the margarine in a 9x13-inch baking pan in the oven. Tilt the pan to coat the bottom. Combine the eggs, sour cream, milk and salt in a bowl and mix well. Stir in the green onions. Pour into the prepared baking pan. Bake for 35 minutes or until the eggs are set.

Variations: May add ½ to 1 cup of your favorite shredded cheese to the egg mixture. For a vegetable version, cover the bottom of the dish with thinly sliced zucchini and half of a red bell pepper, diced. Microwave for 2 to 5 minutes or until tender. Sprinkle with seasoned salt. For a low-fat dish, omit the margarine. Spray the baking pan with nonstick cooking spray and use skim milk. For a small omelet, substitute an 8x8-inch baking dish or a 10-inch round glass dish and use half of the ingredients. Bake for 25 minutes.

Yield: 12 *servings*

The Homeplace

Suzanne and Michael Pescitelli
501 Akron Avenue
Stuart, Florida 34994
(561) 220-9148 or
(800) 251-5473

Come visit this inn with its award-winning restoration, charmingly appointed with antiques and filled with reminiscences of a romantic era. The Homeplace is totally dedicated to guests and gracious hospitality. Guests enjoy a leisurely breakfast, private baths, a lush garden with pool, and a heated spa. It's a haven, which is far too special to be kept secret.

Coconut Grove

Long famous for its unique small town atmosphere, Coconut Grove somehow stands apart in the heart of Miami. It's close to the heart of the city, yet there is a large arts community, fine dining, and unique shops along its tree-lined streets.

Banana Bread French Toast with Fresh Strawberry Syrup

1²/₃ cups sifted flour
³/₄ cup sugar
1 tablespoon baking powder
³/₄ teaspoon salt
3 eggs
¹/₄ cup buttermilk
¹/₃ cup shortening, melted
2 or 3 small bananas, mashed
1¹/₂ cups milk
1 tablespoon butter
Fresh Strawberry Syrup (below)

Preheat the oven to 350 degrees. Combine the flour, sugar, baking powder and ¹/₂ teaspoon of the salt in a bowl and mix well. Combine 1 of the eggs and the buttermilk in a small bowl and mix well. Add the shortening and bananas and mix well. Make a well in the center of the dry ingredients. Pour in the banana mixture. Stir only until moistened. Pour batter into a greased 5x9-inch loaf pan. Bake for 1 hour or until bread tests done. Cool in the pan on a wire rack. Invert onto the wire rack. Cut into thick slices. Combine the remaining 2 eggs, milk and remaining ¹/₄ teaspoon salt in a shallow dish and mix well. Soak the bread slices in the egg mixture. Melt the butter in a heavy skillet. Add the bread slices. Cook the bread until brown on both sides, turning once. Serve with Fresh Strawberry Syrup.

Yield: 6 servings

Fresh Strawberry Syrup

2 cups sugar
2 cups water
4 or 5 strawberries, puréed, strained
1 tablespoon lime juice

Combine the sugar and water in a saucepan. Cover and bring to a boil. Boil for 5 minutes. Add the strawberry purée and lime juice and mix well. Cool, covered, in the refrigerator.

Yield: 2¹/₂ cups

Wild Mushroom Pancakes Drizzled with Balsamic Syrup

Dried wild mushrooms
1 ½ cups sifted flour
1 tablespoon sugar
½ teaspoon baking soda
½ teaspoon salt
2 eggs
1 ½ cups buttermilk
2 tablespoons butter, melted
Balsamic Syrup (below)

Cut the mushrooms with scissors into small pieces. Place mushrooms in a bowl. Cover with water. Soak until reconstituted. Sift the flour, sugar, baking soda and salt together in a bowl. Make a well in the center. Combine the eggs and buttermilk in a bowl and mix well. Add to the dry ingredients and mix until smooth. Stir in the melted butter. Drain the mushrooms and pat dry. Fold the mushrooms into the pancake batter. Pour ¼ cup batter at a time onto a hot lightly greased griddle. Bake until brown on both sides. Serve with Balsamic Syrup.

Yield: 6 servings

Balsamic Syrup

2 cups sugar
2 cups water
1 teaspoon grated lemon rind
Balsamic vinegar to taste

Combine the sugar, water, lemon rind and vinegar in a saucepan. Cover and bring to a boil. Boil for 5 minutes. Strain out the lemon rind if desired. Cool, covered, in the refrigerator.

Yield: 2 ½ cups

**Coconut Grove
Bed & Breakfast**

Annette Rawlings and William Grier
4286 Douglas Road
Miami, Florida 33233
(305) 665-2274 or
(800) 339-9430

This turn-of-the-century home has recently been fully restored, bringing it to the highest standards of luxury. Light-filled, spacious, and airy, all three suites are located on the second floor. Enjoy a full gourmet breakfast daily and a guest membership to an exclusive island resort. Just a short walk to Coconut Grove with its quaint village atmosphere, it is Miami's most convenient location.

The Florida Keys

Florida fades into the Gulf of Mexico like a long beautiful memory. The Overseas Highway travels 150 miles of roads and bridges, and, every inch of the way, encompasses magnificent scenery—crystal, blue-green waters, mangrove forests, and seagrass beds. It would just fade into one last sunset if not for Key West at its southernmost tip. Eccentric, irreverent, and full of seafaring history, Key West offers nightlife, excitement, and a celebration of that sunset each evening in Mallory Square.

The
Florida Keys

Key West

In the 1830s, when wrecking dominated Key West's economy and made the city one of the richest in America, Mallory Square and its old wooden piers were the focal point of that business. Today the square is the spot to be each evening for the nightly ritual of applauding sunset. Mingle with the creative and the crazy at the ceremony only found in Key West!

Aunt Sally's Key Lime Pie

4 eggs, separated
½ cup Key lime juice
1 (14-ounce) can sweetened
    condensed milk
1 (8-inch) graham cracker pie
    shell
¼ teaspoon cream of tartar
⅓ cup sugar

Preheat the oven to 350 degrees. Beat the egg yolks in a bowl until light and thick. Add the lime juice and condensed milk and mix well. Pour into the pie shell. Beat the egg whites and cream of tartar in a mixer bowl until soft peaks form. Add the sugar gradually, beating until stiff peaks form. Spread the egg whites over top sealing to the edge. Bake for 20 minutes or until golden brown. Chill, covered, before serving.

Yield: 6 servings

Orange Cranberry Muffins

1 cup chopped cranberries
¾ cup sugar
2 cups sifted enriched flour
¾ teaspoon baking soda
¼ teaspoon salt
1 egg, beaten
¾ cup orange juice
¼ cup vegetable oil

Preheat the oven to 400 degrees. Combine the cranberries and ½ cup of the sugar in a bowl. Toss to coat the cranberries. Sift the flour, baking soda, salt and the remaining ¼ cup sugar together in a bowl. Combine the egg, orange juice and oil in a small bowl and mix well. Make a well in the dry ingredients. Pour the egg mixture into the dry ingredients. Stir until moistened. Fold in the cranberry mixture. Fill 12 greased muffin cups ⅔ full. Bake for 20 minutes.

Yield: 12 muffins

The Curry Mansion Inn

Al and Edith Amsterdam
511 Caroline Street
Key West, Florida 33040
(305) 294-5349 or
(800) 253-3466

The Curry Mansion Inn, formerly a Victorian masterpiece museum, is now a guesthouse and has been voted "Key West's Best" and one of "10 Best Bed-and-Breakfasts in the U.S." You'll find romantic air-conditioned rooms with private baths, fans, and hand-sewn quilts. Other amenities include breakfast, daily cocktail party, pool, and private Beach Club. The inn is within walking distance to everything—art, antiques, and architecture. It is elegant but relaxed.

Key West is the last stop at the southern tip of America. Originally called Cayo Hueso, or "Island of Bones," Key West was first settled in the early to mid-1800s by a variety of people from New England, Cuba, and the Bahamas, who found an idyllic setting to live and work as fishermen, ship-builders, wreckers, cigar-makers, and spongers. The incredible diversity of these original settlers produced an equally different array of architecture. Key West's Historic District, on the National Register of Historic Places, contains more than 3,000 structures.

Poppy Seed Cake

1 cup butter
1½ cups sugar
4 egg yolks
1 teaspoon baking soda
1 cup sour cream
½ cup chopped walnuts
2 cups sifted flour
1 teaspoon vanilla extract
1 can poppy seeds
4 egg whites, beaten to soft peaks
Cream Cheese Frosting (below)

Preheat the oven to 350 degrees. Cream the butter, sugar and egg yolks in a mixer bowl until light and fluffy. Combine the baking soda and sour cream in a bowl and mix well. Dust the walnuts lightly in the flour. Add the sour cream mixture to the creamed mixture and blend thoroughly. Add the vanilla and mix well. Add the walnuts, flour and poppy seeds and mix well. Fold in the egg whites. Pour into a greased tube pan. Bake for 1 hour or until the cake tests done. Cool in the pan for 10 minutes. Invert onto a serving plate. Frost with Cream Cheese Frosting.

Yield: 15 servings

Cream Cheese Frosting

3 ounces cream cheese, softened
1½ cups confectioners' sugar
1 teaspoon vanilla extract

Combine the cream cheese, confectioners' sugar and vanilla in a bowl and mix well.

Yield: 1½ cups

Margaritas

1 (6-ounce) can limeade
6 ounces triple sec
6 ounces golden tequila
1 ½ cups water
Lime slices
Salt

Combine the limeade, triple sec, tequila and water in a container with a tightfitting lid. Cover and shake well. Squeeze the juice from a lime slice on the rim of a glass. Dip in salt. Place squeezed lime slice in bottom of glass. Add ice cubes. Pour margarita over ice.

Yield: 8 drinks

Watson House
Ed Czaplicki and Joe Beres
525 Simonton Street
Key West, Florida 33040
(305) 294-6712 or
(800) 621-9405

Watson House is a small, award-winning inn with just three units. It features a heated pool and whirlpool spa, decks, and gardens. All units have their own distinct style, private baths, color television, air conditioning, and telephones. Larger suites have full kitchens. Continental breakfast is served each morning. Privacy prevails in this adults-only establishment.

Index

Inn Route of Florida • P.O. Box 6187 • Palm Harbor, Florida 34684

Send _____ copies of *From Muffins To Margaritas* @ $18.95 ea. $ _____

Shipping and Handling @ $3.50 ea. $ _____

Total $ _____

Method of Payment:

[   ] VISA

[   ] MasterCard

[   ] Discover

[   ] American Express

[   ] Check payable to Inn Route

Name _____

Address _____

City _____ State _____ Zip _____

Account Number _____ Expiration Date _____

Signature _____   *Photocopies accepted.*